BACK ROADS LORE

VOLUME 1
BEYOND THE BLACKTOP
LEWIS - WEATHERLY - NELSON

Eerie Lights Publishing
Eerielights.com
Eerielightspublishing.com

BACK ROADS LORE

VOLUME 1
BEYOND THE BLACKTOP
LEWIS - WEATHERLY - NELSON

Based on travel, interviews, and research conducted by the Back Roads Lore team.

ISBN: 978-1-945950-45-2

Back Roads Lore
Backroadslore.com

EERIE LIGHTS
Eerie Lights Publishing
Eerielights.com
Eerielightspublishing.com

Cover art by Kevin Lee Nelson

Editor: Jerry Hajewski

Book layout/design: SMAK
smakgraphics.com

TABLE OF CONTENTS

Introduction

Welcome to the first issue of Back Roads Lore (BRL). This story began nearly twenty years ago when Back Roads Lore started out as a small collective of like-minded researchers with a simple mission to chronicle anomalous events, Fortean mysteries, urban legends, and strange folklore. As the name implies, we put special emphasis on legends that are off the beaten track. After many years of investigating countless cases we decided the best way to share our ongoing research was by publishing a journal documenting our adventures, discoveries, and new areas of research.

The primary goal of this journal is to present extraordinary stories that are relatively unknown, forgotten, or very recent and newsworthy. We will generally avoid articles on popular legends that already have mountains of published research. Back Roads Lore will also explore new theories, examine unconventional concepts, and provide deep dives into the nature of mysterious encounters and events of high-strangeness. Generally speaking, attempting to prove or disprove the existence of various creatures, cryptids, or ghosts is not the goal of our research; rather, we prefer to present the facts, history, and lore, along with objective critical analysis, so that readers can make up their own mind and decide what they believe is probable or real. In short, amazing stories can speak for themselves.

Each issue of Back Roads Lore will follow a general theme. This inaugural issue's theme is *Beyond the Blacktop*. Therefore, each article in this issue deals with legends that exist outside the safe confines of suburbia and well-traveled roads. You can also expect exciting travelogues documenting specific expeditions and on-the-road observations from some of our more wild adventures. Additionally, each issue will also have an on-going column section. Our initial columns are: *The Mysterious Outdoors, The Digital Campfire, Ghost Town Gazetteer, The Offbeat Track, Behind This Curtain* and, *I Dare You*.

The Mysterious Outdoors will provide commentary and analysis on legends associated with wilderness areas, parks, summer camps, and other back country sites. *The Digital Campfire* will examine how contemporary folklore is developing and evolving on the Internet and discuss new technological trends, digital cryptids, monstrous memes, and emergent crowd-sourced legends. *Ghost Town Gazetteer* will explore the legends and lore of long abandoned towns around the country.

America's back-roads are full of peculiar establishments attempting to lure in curious travelers. In *Behind This Curtain*, we'll take a look at curious museums, strange collections, bizarre shops, and other fascinating stops. The *Offbeat Track* will feature a particular roadside oddity or attraction. Whether it's a bizarre roadside landmark, or an abandoned amusement park we'll give you the scoop. Lastly, *I Dare You* will challenge readers to interact with specific legends and sites through ritualistic engagement, allowing intrepid adventurers to actually take part in a legend's tradition.

With rare exception, we always make sure to visit the actual locations of the legends we research. One of the core tenets of Back Roads Lore is to get out there and experience these legendary and infamous places firsthand. It also allows the opportunity to interview witnesses and locals and to better understand the perspectives of those personally affected by strange events. We aim to minimize so-called "armchair research," as there is no substitute for actual field experience and on-site observation.

Lastly, many local legends and curious bits of regional lore are at risk of vanishing within a generation if they are not recorded and preserved. In the past, people kept unusual local tales alive mostly through oral traditions, often through storytelling at the local tavern or by passing strange cautionary tales down to their children. Unfortunately, in today's highly-mobile society and increasingly isolating culture, most people are generally unaware of the colorful and rich folklore of their own area. Unique history and folklore is something that should be documented and celebrated, as they play an important part of our cultural heritage. Therefore, it is our hope that Back Roads Lore will fulfill a necessary role by discovering endangered lore and preserving it for future generations.

— Back Roads Lore Crew

The Mysterious Outdoors:
Strange Things in the Shawnee Forest
By David Weatherly

Southern Illinois's Shawnee National Forest is a 289,000-acre park located in the Ozark and Shawnee hills. The park's headquarters is located in the city of Harrisburg, and the forest itself sprawls through several counties. The park is the largest publicly owned piece of land in the state of Illinois.

The park was designated the Shawnee National Forest in 1939 by then President Franklin D. Roosevelt. The forest is rich in hardwood trees, and throughout the 1930s and 1940s, the Civilian Conservation Corps planted large tracts of pine trees to help prevent erosion and rebuild the soil.

While not as high profile as many other national parks, the Shawnee site is considered a true gem by many locals and it's a popular destination for hiking and other outdoor activities. But if you're planning on visiting the park, there may be more to see than lush forest and abundant wildlife. Strange things have been reported from the Shawnee National Forest. With its dark night skies, the site is a great place to star gaze and some people doing so have seen more than just stars and planets.

On February 1, 2020, three people in the Shawnee Forest observed a series of strange objects in the sky at around 7:30 in the evening.

The trio were camping on a bluff about three hundred feet in elevation. One of the campers spotted the objects and pointed them out to the others. Initially, the objects appeared to be stars, but as the campers watched, the cluster moved east across the sky. They were spaced out evenly and moved in a pattern with one of the lights in front and higher, apparently leading the other two. The lights did not twinkle or flash as they moved.

One of the campers filed a report with the NUFORC (National UFO Reporting Center) and noted:

"They were definitely part of an intentional formation. We had a clear view of the sky, clear night, no clouds, and no light pollution. I was completely sober and saw this clearly. I fly drones and this was not a drone similar to commercial consumer drones. There were no anti-aircraft lights or red lights resembling a military operation."

The witnesses watched the objects for about ten minutes until they finally faded out one by one.

While the account is interesting, a report from 2003 is even more curious. Two campers hiked into the Shawnee Forest for a getaway on June 24. They'd gotten a late start and by the time they had their camp and tent set up at their "usual spot," it was one o'clock at night. The pair turned in to get some sleep, but a quiet rest wasn't in the cards that night. The reporting witness told the NUFORC:

"After a few minutes, my camping partner wakes me up to a light about 30 feet away. The light beings were moving, and we then see two more lights but smaller on each side of the center larger light. Then we were just totally astonished to realize that we were seeing a tiny little craft floating gently around like a dragonfly and always shining those three pale orange-colored lights directly at us."

According to the witness's report, the craft was round, about the size of a tire, and moved like a dragonfly while emitting the orange lights.

The witness says that the craft flew around the campsite for about an hour. The whole time the orange lights pulsated, though sometimes the lights got darker. Both campers fell asleep while the strange little craft was in the camp.

I received a brief but very odd report from a woman who told me that she and her boyfriend had seen "some kind of alien-looking thing" while driving near the Shawnee in the 1980s.

The witness, Jillian, told me that it was sometime in September 1983 and she and her then boyfriend had been out for a day hike in the Shawnee. She says they ended up just sitting in the car talking for a while before they left to drive back home. Traveling along the border of the park with the sun going down, the pair were shocked when a creature appeared on the road ahead. Jillian described the thing to me:

"It was on two legs, about five feet tall and very pale gray-green in color. It was naked but I couldn't tell if it was male or female. It had a bulbous head, like, it was big headed on the top, only the facial features were small, so the head looked even more out of size."

Jillian's boyfriend, who was driving, stopped the car and the couple stared at the thing for a moment. It had come from the right side of the road and stopped, looking directly at the oncoming vehicle. After just a few seconds, the creature turned, "leapt into the woods" and vanished.

Jillian and her boyfriend broke up soon afterwards and she says that she has avoided the park ever since the incident.

But these accounts are pale in comparison to a bizarre encounter from 1970.

Around 8:30 in the evening on April 10 a man was driving along the perimeter of the park when his car engine suddenly died. The puzzled man tried to restart the car, but there wasn't a spark of life in the engine.

The man climbed out of his vehicle, intending to inspect the engine to see if he could fix the problem, but before he could investigate the matter, he was violently attacked.

But it wasn't a wild animal from the forest; rather, the man was assaulted by a "six-foot-tall, black humanoid with greenish glowing almond shaped eyes."

The thing knocked the man to the ground and the pair began to wrestle and the man found himself fighting for his life. The creature, he reported, appeared cat-like, and gave off a "musty odor."

The witness was saved when the headlights of an approaching truck frightened the cat creature, causing it to abandon the attack and flee from the scene, vanishing into the forest.

The distressed man had suffered superficial wounds from the clawed creature and was naturally shaken up by the whole experience.

The account was originally reported in Jerome Clark and Loren Coleman's *Creatures on the Outer Edge*.

It should be noted that these reports are only the tip of the iceberg when it comes to strange things in the Shawnee National Forest. There are also reports of Bigfoot lurking in the woods, dogmen, ghosts, and rumors of a weird vortex. With all these and other stories, there's more than just a slice of nature to explore in the Illinois forest.

The Mysterious Outdoors: Strange Things in the Shawnee Forest By David Weatherly

The Digital Campfire:
Who or What is Loab?
By Kevin Lee Nelson

In April of 2022 Swedish musician and digital artist, Steph Maj Swanson, who goes by the user-name Supercomposite on Twitter (now 'X') , made a startling discovery. She was experimenting with "negative prompt weights" in the AI-generated art program DALL-E 2. Negative prompts are a way of removing unwanted image material by creating their opposite. She used the negative prompt "Brando::-1" to see how the program would interpret the opposite of Marlon Brando. What it came up with was an image of a weird skyline logo with the nonsensical text "DIGITA PNTICS." Swanson wondered if the opposite of the image, in turn, would to be a picture of Marlon Brando. She entered the words "DIGITA PNTICS skyline logo::-1." What she got back was something completely unexpected and very disturbing.

Instead of getting a picture of Marlon Brando, or even something like Marlon Brando, she got an image of a strange, pock-faced, haggard woman. She attempted the experiment a number of times, but the results were similar. She wrote on Twitter, "I received these off-putting images, all of the same devastated-looking older woman with defined triangles of rosacea(?) on her cheeks." Swanson decided to name the strange woman "Loab" after the word appeared within one of the AI-generated images. Swanson wrote, "I discovered this woman, who I call Loab, in April. The AI reproduced her more easily than most celebrities. Her presence is persistent, and she haunts every image she touches."

Swanson then tried to create new images using Loab as a base. However, it didn't seem to matter what other images she combined; if Loab was part of the mix, the results were always unsettling and nightmarish, like something rotten in the stew. She said, "Through some kind of emergent statistical accident, something about this woman is adjacent to extremely gory and macabre imagery in the distribution of the AI's world knowledge." Swanson noticed that certain prominent features were preserved when crossing Loab images with avatars, animals, and even when combining 3-4 images at a time. Eventually she was able to generate images that did not contain Loab, but when she combined these seemingly innocuous images together, Loab reappeared. Swanson compared the Loab to a *dominant gene* in the latent space.

You might be asking, *What is the "latent space"?* In artificial intelligence latent space refers to an abstract multi-dimensional mathematical space that maps what a neural network has learned from training images. In the most simplistic definition, the latent space is a mathematical representation of data where similar items with strong associations are grouped together. Swanson says, "The latent space is kind of like you're exploring a map of different concepts in the AI. A prompt is like an arrow that tells you how far to walk in this concept map and in which direction." She speculated that the latent space region of the AI map where Loab lives, in addition to being in close proximity to macabre imagery, must be isolated enough that any image aggregation requests are only able to use Loab from her area and no related images due to its isolation in that part of the latent space.

Loab has been called "first AI-generated cryptid." Some futurist thinkers have theorized that intelligences, artificial or otherwise, inhabit the dark corners of the latent space. They see it as a digital frontier with its own digital fauna and flora, and even its own demons. Perhaps there are entities that have always existed that are now able to show themselves, or even communicate, via AI technology. After the discovery of Loab went viral, an entire mythos has developed around her, and other artists are encountering their own Loab images and messages. As more artists contribute to the library of Loab images, other AI systems will use those images as a part of their latent space map, giving Loab an even stronger presence and expand her reach. According to Swanson, "If we want to get rid of her, it's already too late."

Stay Away From Haunchyville
By Chad Lewis

Step right up folks! Grab your popcorn, peanuts, and some fresh-squeezed lemonade because the circus is coming to town. Except this isn't your normal circus, because this odd circus has no wild and exotic animals, no silly clowns throwing confetti, no majestic ringmaster leading the show, not even one game of skill can be found. Believe it or not, this circus doesn't even have a big top. If you are a bit confused, don't worry, you should be. Let me introduce you to the hidden village of circus performers called Haunchyville!

The legend of Haunchyville began decades ago with the story of a large group of circus performers who were spending the off-seasons in the comfort and warmth of the Florida sun. Their cozy village consisted of several dozen little people (dwarfs) who were under the employment of a spiteful and abusive circus manager. After years of being mistreated, the performers had finally reached their limit and decided to put a permanent end to their tormenter. A sinister plan was hatched, and soon their horrible manager was no longer among the living. Fresh on the lam from the law, and seeking a better life for themselves, the little people decided that Wisconsin would be far enough away to ensure their safety. Luckily, the small town of Muskego had the perfect hiding spot. Situated down a long dead-end road, tucked tight against a lake and hidden within a thick forest, their new home even came with a large cornfield that was perfect for concealing the property. The patch of land on Mystic Road provided the perfect mix of seclusion and privacy that the little people were searching for.

Over the years, the new residents sparked a never-ending stream of curiosity from the locals who had dubbed the place Haunchyville. Tales sprung up of a peculiar village of little people lurking in the woods. Wild speculation about the newcomers floated through the region, and with each telling, the story became more absurd. Seeking to live quietly along the idyllic lakeview property, the newcomers were plagued by curious sightseers and drunken teenagers hellbent on discovering the "Haunchies." The never-ending parade of visitors forced the group to hire an average sized man to vigilantly watch over the property. Armed with his trusty shotgun, the attentive watchman was said to greet any encroaching visitor with a shoot first and ask questions later approach. To make matters more puzzling, no one could agree on just what the Haunchies were actually doing on their property. Versions of the Haunchies' day-to-day activities varied widely. Some tales told of them living a peaceful subsistence life of farming, while others claimed that strange occult activity could be heard emanating from the property. Outside of the most prevalent explanation (and most believable), that the little people were simply retired circus performers, other origin stories of Haunchyville were much more bizarre. In 2004, the August 27 edition of the *Capital Times*, the newspaper included an even more fantastical origin story of Haunchyville, claiming "a farmer tore up a tree and hundreds of little people came pouring out." This incredible theory seems to follow in the belief that the little circus people were more of the fairy or gnome type, rather than old carnival workers looking to spend their golden years in Wisconsin. Even though gnome sightings are not uncommon in the state, most witnesses that have had a run-in with the Haunchies firmly believe that they are human.

Because the area is so secluded, far from the prying eyes of any adults or law enforcement, it provides the ideal location for a lovers' lane. After the Haunchies moved in, teenagers who went parking out in the area reported being attacked by mysterious little creatures that were lurking in the darkness. If you were brave enough, or foolish enough, to venture out there, it was said that the Haunchies would chase you away from their property. They were armed with knives, baseball bats, pitchforks or worse. In their wonderful book *Weird Wisconsin*, Rick Hendricks and Linda Godfrey included a story from a man who had grown up in the area. The creepy tale this man had always heard involved two young teenagers who drove out to Haunchyville to "get to know one another" at the lovers' lane. Not long after they arrived, they were attacked by the vicious little people. The next day, law enforcement discovered the couple's mutilated bodies still inside their car. The only clues to their murder were several small scratch marks on the roof of their vehicle indicating the presence of small creatures. Obviously, the story of the dead teenagers was heavily influenced, or most likely conflated, with the well-known Hook Man urban legend. Undoubtedly, these curious stories only prompted more people to visit the site and the strange circle of weirdness fed itself.

The same abovementioned *Capital Times* article also told this following popular cautionary legend about Haunchyville, claiming that, "a homeless man was found strung up in a barn with hundreds of baby-sized footprints in the dirt beneath him." Apparently, a strange note left beneath his rotting corpse warned others of what would happen if they too moseyed into Haunchyville. To this day, it is said that you can see the pitiful ghost of the hanging man dangling from the side of the barn, acting like some sort of demented scarecrow, forever tasked with keeping away any unwanted visitors. Curiously, many of the reports I currently get from people visiting Haunchyville tell of ghostly activity happening on the property.

As you might expect from a village of little people, everything in Haunchyville is said to be tiny-sized. Those who visit the area report seeing waist-high stop signs placed on the roads by the Haunchies. Other visitors claim to have spotted smaller-sized homes and stores dotting the landscape. Thin trails will lead you to the water where you will see tiny-sized boats pulled up along the shoreline. Behind all of the legends, the idea exists that Haunchyville is a perfect oasis for any below average height person.

One of the most tantalizing aspects of Haunchyville is the average-sized protector that is said to be responsible for patrolling the village, keeping its privacy-craving inhabitants safe, and making sure that any unwanted visitors get the message that they are not welcome. I have been unable to dig up anything about his origin or story. Does he also reside in the area? Is he related to the Haunchies? Maybe he is just a hired hand who is sympathetic to their pursuit of happiness. A September 13, 2005, article in the *Journal Times*, provided a tad more detail into the dangerous side of Haunchyville, claiming the Haunchies were described as being "Mean… they chase away trespassers with knives …or……an average-sized gun-toting bodyguard blasts you full of birdshot if you wander into the land of little." I have personally spoken with a witness who told me that while he and friends were out trying to locate the village, someone blasted at their car with pellets. Unfortunately, the terrified group did not stick around long enough to see who was wielding the weapon. Whoever or whatever this strange protector is, he seems to be an expert in evading the police, as no one has ever been questioned or arrested for shooting at people in Haunchyville.

The only problem with the amazing legend is that by all accounts, Haunchyville has never existed in any form whatsoever. No murderous little people, no peaceful farmers, no shotgun wielding guard. The entirety of the Haunchyville legend seems to be nothing more than a wonderfully strange urban legend. The legend itself dates back to at least the 1950s, and quite possibly even further into history. Even the etymology of "Haunchyville" is shrouded in mystery. No one has been able to find any explanation as to how it came to be known by this unusual name. Perhaps it is just a nonsensical word that sounded really cool and eerie. I have been unable to dig up anything that might even provide where the spark to ignite the legend originated. I could understand how a story might evolve if a married dwarf couple moved to a home in the woods back in the 1950s, but, alas, we don't even have that. This lack of any compelling evidence only adds to the mystery and intrigue of Haunchyville. Some speculate that the whole thing is more supernatural in nature, and that the Haunchies, along with their overzealous guard, are not actually there in the way we think of other residents being there. Several well-worn explanations have sprung up to explain the anomaly which is Haunchyville. Arguably, the most popular is that the whole village of Haunchyville is composed of ghosts and spirits. This would help explain why no evidence of any buildings, people, or graves has ever been located. If, say, a person is tuned in to the right frequency or is of a psychic bent, they might be able to experience Haunchyville, while others are left wondering why a solitary cornfield is so spooky. Others contend that perhaps Haunchyville is an out-of-place place---meaning that it is an outlier from some other time, dimension, or existence. All of these fascinating explanations also cover for the fact that Haunchyville is only sporadically experienced.

The realness of Haunchyville can be debated all day long, but what can't be disputed are the hordes of people who have come away from their Haunchyville visit with nothing more than an expensive trespassing ticket. One local police officer estimated the number of trespassing citations issued over the last few decades to be in the hundreds. The land on which Haunchyville is said to exist is also under attack by suburban development. As more and more of the untouched nature area is sold off for large family homes, the alleged site of Haunchyville shrinks. My first visit in search of Haunchyville occurred about 25 years ago. Back then the place had a desolate and forlorn appearance that gave a visitor the idea that anything was possibly hiding among the wilds. I must have somehow overlooked all of the No Trespassing signs, or perhaps they were not plastered out there yet. On subsequent visits over the decades, that magical feeling I had that something otherworldly existed—concealed by the environment or the occult—started to dissipate as more and more homes encroached on the area. Again, the No Trespassing signs must have somehow disappeared from my view. My most recent visit took place during the summer of 2023, and I was saddened to see that the alleged village of Haunchyville had once again shrunk in size of its heyday.

Yet, somehow, against all odds, the legend of Haunchyville is still alive and well. Today, I receive no fewer requests for directions to the mysterious place than I did 20 years ago. Not only does the legend of Haunchyville survive, plenty of people are still reporting encounters with the Haunchies and their aggressive protector. A simple internet search will provide you with numerous accounts of strange encounters with the Haunchies.

As weird as the folklore of Haunchyville is, Wisconsin is not alone in housing this type of peculiar legend. There are several similarly constructed legends of towns throughout the US where smaller sized people are said to be dwelling in secrecy. In Ohio, legend trippers head off in search of "Midgettown" and "Munchkinland," where the diminutively sized residents are said to throw rocks at any pesky outsiders. In New Jersey, having just one puzzling "Midgetville" is not enough. The state boasts numerous locations that are touted as being the home of these enigmatic residents. In Virginia, curious travelers lament the destruction of their "Midgetville." I am continually captivated by our fascination with these types of places. Since most of the legends span decades, were they perpetuated by Hollywood? Are these stories influenced by the Munchkins from 1939's *Wizard of Oz* movie, or the Oompa Loompas from the Willy Wonka films? Did the gradual decline of the prevalence of circuses in America help fuel the creation of such mysterious towns and villages? In one hundred years from now, will we still be telling tales of little people living among the shadows, or is this something stuck in a certain time and era? Unfortunately, there are no simple answers as to why Haunchyville and other weird places continue to puzzle and fascinate us.

Although my travels down Mystic Road ended with no village of little people, no dilapidated miniature homes, and (luckily) no trigger-fingered gatekeeper, I still hold out hope that Haunchyville is still out there, still waiting for the right person to wander by, and I sincerely hope that future generations of legend hunters continue to search for this magical place.

Resources and Works Consulted:

Hendricks, Richard & Godfrey, Linda. *Weird Wisconsin*. Barnes & Noble Books. 2005.

Journal Times. September 13, 2005.

The Capital Times. August 27, 2004.

Stay Away From Haunchyville By Chad Lewis

The Hebron Ghost Light
By David Weatherly

July 16, 1952. Just before midnight on a dusty road in the small town of Hebron, Maryland, a pair of state police officers are on patrol. The night is clear but steamy as the officers turn onto Church Street Extended, a mile long stretch of road lined by trees on both sides. In the distance, the officers see something strange—a circular ball of yellow light floating just above the road. The yellow orb is moving toward the police car, and as the officers continue to drive forward, the light moves forward as well, approaching rapidly in the middle of the road straight toward the patrol car. At the last possible moment, the trooper behind the wheel swerves off the road, narrowly avoiding a collision with the oncoming light. The patrol car skids to a stop on the shoulder of the road and the two stunned officers watch as the light stops as well, hovering in the road about twenty feet from the vehicle.

As the orb hovers in the glare of the car's headlights, the trooper restarts the vehicle and begins driving toward the light again. This time, the orb retreats, racing away from the patrol car. The trooper speeds up in an attempt to overtake the light, but it stays just ahead of the car, matching the officer's speed and staying at a distance. When the police car hits about forty miles per hour on the dirt road, the light suddenly vanishes.

The officers had just encountered the Hebron Ghost Light.

The town of Hebron, Maryland, is in Wicomico County in an area of the state commonly referred to as the Eastern Shore. Hebron is now considered part of the Salisbury, Maryland-Delaware Metropolitan Statistical Area. According to the 2020 census, the town itself has 1,113 residents.

What is commonly called Ghost Light Road is just off Route 50 between the towns of Hebron and Mardella Springs, formerly called "Old Railroad Road." My colleague Dale Kaczmarek of the Ghost Research Society found during his research that sightings of the light most frequently occurred between Portermill Road exactly one mile south of Route 50 and Church Street Extended, another half mile south.

It's unknown exactly when the light first started manifesting on the road but according to locals, by the time the ghost light hit the news in 1952, it had already been appearing for almost half a century. This would put the first sightings of the orb circa 1877.

If accurate, the timing would indicate that when the ghost light first started appearing, the area was nothing more than scattered farms. A more likely scenario is that the legend of the light developed sometime after 1890; that's when the Baltimore, Chesapeake and Atlantic Railroad was extended westward from Salisbury. The railroad crossed an old country road where there was a general store, an old colonial era home, a few farms, and lots of woods. The railroad designated the location a shipping point and dubbed it Hebron after the Biblical city. In short order, a lumber plant was built, and the town began to grow and develop.

Depot, Hebron, Md.

By the 1920s, Hebron was a hub for manufacturing with several shirt factories, a canning operation, flour mill and lumber mill all in operation as well as a bustling farming community growing a range of crops.

I'll note here that I have a personal connection to the Hebron ghost light—namely, family who grew up in the area—some of whom still live there. It was also one of the first legends I remember hearing about when I was a young boy, so in that sense, it's an important part of my fascination with the strange. Over the years, hearing stories about the light from family and friends, it has always come to mind whenever accounts of ghost lights arise. The legend is now forgotten by many, though it's often found in books about hauntings in the region, and local newspapers sometimes resurrect it around Halloween season if they run an article on local ghost stories.

My mother told me that she remembered the ghost light well, noting: "It was around in my days, and in my dad's days. A bunch of us went several times at night and sat along ghost light road waiting for it, but we never saw it."

Plenty of other people in the area did spot the light. My mother recalled a story about a pair of men who tried to catch the light by playing chicken with it in the 1940s: "In dad's day, two guys sat in their cars at each end of the road and waited for it to appear. When it did, they each drove toward it, and it disappeared."

The men narrowly avoided having a head-on collision when the light vanished. They apparently didn't attempt the stunt again. They walked away without an explanation as to what the light was. Being confounded by the light certainly wasn't limited to locals. The two state police officers who'd had such a close encounter with the light couldn't explain it either.

Trooper Robert Burkhardt, one of the men on the scene that July night, returned the following evening with five other officers in tow. When the patrolmen arrived, they found that the mysterious light was already present, hovering on Church Street as if waiting for the policemen.

The officers climbed out of their vehicles and tried to surround the glowing orb. The light suddenly blinked out as if something had turned it off. Almost instantly, it reappeared, floating over a nearby field.

Several days later, Officer Edward H. Bracey and other officers pursued the ghost light in vehicles. The officers reached speeds of fifty miles per hour before the light suddenly veered out of the lane and out over a field.

Many of the officers who were sent to investigate the light were skeptical of the story—at least: until they got to the scene and saw the thing for themselves.

When the ghost light hit the news in the 1950s, it was big news for the small community. People all over the country were suddenly interested in the story, though many locals took it in stride.

The July 14, 1952, edition of the *Baltimore Evening Sun* ran a story about the mystery, reporting that residents of Hebron had been spotting the light for years and didn't worry about it: "Old Hebronites feel certain it is connected with the hanging of a man some years back." The paper reported:

"The Hebron light, supernatural or not, was recently given a thorough investigation by a skeptical group of Maryland State policemen. Under the leadership of Lieut. C. C. Serman, of the Salisbury barracks, a number of troopers chased the light.

"The light, according to the police report, bounces along a back road which connects Hebron with United States Route 50. Or rather, it doesn't exactly bounce. But it can disappear from the front of a witness and reappear behind him."

Serman may have been a skeptic initially, but he changed his mind after chasing the light around. He told reporters that the orb resembled a "phosphorescent wash basin."

The *Sun* also noted that the light caused "an uneasy tingling along the nape of the neck."

One old timer in the area said that he'd seen the light off and on for years and that it glowed like a pale-yellow headlight from a 1920s era automobile. He also said that the light would stay stationary unless, or until, something tried to chase it. While such locals had long known about the ghost light, all the media attention brought it to the forefront and there was quite a buzz about the mystery. The fact that police officers had chased the light put even more attention on the mystery and in short order, large groups of curious motorists started showing up along the road, parking at the scene and waiting for the glowing orb to appear.

Nervous local officials wanted the story to go away and took measures to try to put an end to the ghost light by squelching law enforcement involvement. The July 16, 1952, edition of the *Daily Times* out of Salisbury announced:

"In the wake of widespread publicity about the Hebron light, State Police near Salisbury have been advised to release no further information about it.

"According to First Sgt. Thomas E. Veditz, assistant barracks commander, information about the light now has to come from State Police headquarters at Pikesville."

The police may have been muzzled but the mystery didn't just go away. The lack of official explanations likely increased speculation as to the light's origin. In the 1950s, there wasn't as much broad knowledge of ghost light legends as there is today.

While the term ghost light itself is perhaps the most commonly used phrase to designate unexplained atmospheric lights, they are known by a variety of terms including spooklights, will-o-the-whisps, and fairy lights.

Typically, local lore will attach ghost lights to hauntings in the area, the idea being that the light is a wandering spirit that either emits the light due to its unearthly glow, or that it's a spirit carrying a lantern or other light of some kind. Of course, scientists usually claim that the lights are due to some kind of natural phenomena such as gases being produced and released from the environment. When Hebron's mysterious light started getting attention, ghost stories and other explanations quickly arose to explain its origin.

One popular ghost story associated with the light claimed that it was the spirit of an African American slave who had been hung in the woods along the road. His spirit was said to wander the area trying to find his killers and get justice. A variation of the legends says that the ghost light is the spirit of a man who committed suicide in the woods. His death was also by hanging and his remains went undiscovered for many years, his corpse rotting and decaying in the trees.

Yet another version of the tale connects it to a murder, one that resulted from a gambling dispute with the murder victim haunting the road and the woods where he met his end.

It's also common for ghost lights to be connected to railroad legends, and the Hebron light is no exception. One version of the tale claims the ghost light is the lantern of a phantom railroad worker who was killed along tracks in the area. The man was struck by an oncoming train, and since his death, he has continued to wander the area, waving his lantern in his endless task to warn of an approaching train, one that is long gone.

In her book *Haunted Eastern Shore*, author Mindie Burgoyne mentions a variant of the railroad legend, one related in 1970 by Delmar resident Mary Twilley. Twilley recounts:

"Long ago, an argument was going on as to where to build the new railroad, which was to go through Hebron. One particular engineer wanted the tracks to be laid where the Ghost Light Road is today. Instead of laying tracks there, a county road was built instead. It is said that the ghost of this engineer with his ghostly train comes down the Ghost Light Road once in a while. The strange light often seen there is the light in front of his ghostly engine."

Yet another version of the ghost light goes further astray and connects it to a notorious woman named Patty Cannon. Cannon was a slave trader and murderess in the 18th century. She lured her victims to a tavern she owned near the Mason Dixon Line where she robbed and murdered them. Her preferred method of killing was the use of arsenic. Her victims ranged from ages 17 to 50 and there's debate about how many people she actually killed.

Cannon was caught and put on trial, but she cheated the hangman on the night of her execution—she had smuggled in a dose of arsenic, hidden in the hem of her dress, which she used to take her own life.

Legend says Cannon's skull was kept for years at the public library in Dover, Delaware, where it sat quietly in a hatbox. How, or why, her legend ended up tied to Hebron's ghost light isn't clear but nevertheless, a few tales link the light to her nasty spirit.

An even stranger version of the ghost light was shared with me by an old friend named Derke who grew up in the area in the 1970s/80s. The tale revolves around a boogeyman, or rather, boogeywoman, figure who carried a lantern. The figure was an old woman who would put her rocking chair in the middle of the road and sit a lantern down beside it. The ghostly old woman punished children who "refused to take their medicine."

In some versions, the bouncing light was the woman walking along the road or sitting in her rocking chair holding the light as she rocked. Other versions say the old woman carried the children away and they would never be seen again.

Some theories weren't ghost related and were completely absurd. One suggestion was that the glowing orb was created by light being reflected off of a piece of glass—a piece of glass that was being carried across low hanging branches by a raccoon or opossum! How or why the animal did this on numerous occasions was never explained.

There were, of course, more logic-based theories suggested to explain the light. Several people posited that there was some unique quality in the dust of the old, original road. When vehicles caused the dust to kick up, a reflection was created in the headlights, creating the illusion of a spectral, glowing orb. While the theory was interesting, it didn't explain the ability of the light to move around outside of the direction headlights were pointed. It's also important to note that locals said the light had first appeared well before electricity and modern vehicles were traveling the route. Early witnesses reported that they first thought the light was someone carrying a lantern down the road. The light was also seen moving through the thick trees lining the road early on.

It should come as no surprise that skeptics came out of the woodwork to "explain" the light to those who had seen it. Showing their arrogance, most of the experts commented on the mystery from afar. Baltimore's so-called "leading ghost-debunker," Dr. H.C. McComas, laughed the whole story off and fed the *Baltimore Sun* a series of smart-alecky remarks about the ghostly orb, stating: "That sounds like what we call a "psychic light." Used to carry one around in my pocket" (*Baltimore Evening Sun*, July 14, 1952).

McComas was a former professor and considered himself an expert debunker. He apparently couldn't even be bothered with the Hebron mystery. He told the paper: "In running down these things, you never find that the facts correspond with the stories." McComas didn't run anything down though. If he had bothered to look, he would have discovered all the police officers—trained observers—who'd had puzzling experiences on Ghost Light Road.

One professor from John Hopkins University (who did not want his identity released to the public) said that the ghost light was nothing more than a "mobile concentration of marsh gas."

The July 16, 1952, edition of Salisbury's *Daily Times* carried the story under the headline "Professor Believes Ghost Light Is Gas." The unidentified man stated:

"There must be a marsh out there, or perhaps a peat bog. The gas is generated by decaying vegetable matter; it seeps up to the surface, gathers in a sort of pocket and is moved around by gusts of wind."

Just like McComas, the anonymous professor hadn't even bothered to visit the location of the sightings; rather, he sat in his office and cleared the mystery up with a proclamation about marsh gas. For its part, the Times did point out that the expert opinion had some flaws:

"The professor's explanation wouldn't seem to cover some reports of the behavior of the Hebron Light.

"Marsh gas could scarcely be expected to indulge in bursts of speed up to 50 miles per hour and sudden change of direction such as some observers have reported."

Some scientists travel to Hebron to investigate the mystery. One group spent some time along the road and came to the conclusion that the light was nothing more than swamp gas. These experts seemed to have missed one important fact—there was no swamp where the light was appearing!

Locals didn't think much of the scientific explanations either. My father, who was fairly skeptical of things of a ghostly nature, recalled the ghost light well. Although he wasn't sure what to make of it, he didn't think much of the scientific investigation either and he recalled the visit:

"Some big wigs came along with a whole bunch of fancy equipment and said they were going to study the light and figure out what it was. They sat around out there and did all kinds of tests. They couldn't figure it out, so they just said it was swamp gas and left."

Some who came to look for the light just wanted evidence. A photographer from *Life* magazine tried to capture the ghost light on film during the summer of 1952. The July 14 edition of Salisbury's *Daily Times* reported on the attempt.

"A *Life* magazine photographer who hoped to return to his Washington office with evidence of the mystifying 'ghost light' which haunts a Hebron woods road failed to get a picture.

"Albert Fenn of *Life* came well-armed with a variety of cameras to catch the sight. But no light appeared Saturday night. He and State Trooper Robert W. Burkhardt, who has seen the mystery glow on several occasions, kept an all-night vigil."

Robert Burkhardt, who had seen and chased the light several times during the heydays of the summer of 1952, remained puzzled by the thing even in his later years. After he retired from law enforcement, he was reluctant to talk about Hebron's Ghost Light and he recalled it as one of the strangest and most difficult episodes of his career. Burkhardt recalled:

"It was just like a neon tube when you turned it out. It faded slowly into a reddish glow which finally went out" (Gaddis, *Mysterious Fires and Lights*).

The ghost light was in the media for about two weeks after the initial incident with police officers, a long time for something to hold the attention of reporters. The story was likely quirky enough that editors thought it would have human interest appeal. News hounds from several big city papers made their way to the rural town to cover the story, using it to fill the summer news drought.

There was a brief resurgence of reports of the light in the 1970s, but this didn't last long and beyond this, sightings of the light have been very sporadic and few and far between and there have not been any reports in recent years. Many people say that the light stopped appearing when alterations were made to the road itself. At one point, the road was paved with oyster shells, but this didn't deter the light's activity. According to records at the Wicomico County Road Division, the road was tarred and chipped in 1953, and in 1958 it was widened and rebuilt. In 1974 the road was blacktopped and by many accounts, this put a stop to the manifestations of the light.

Despite the ghost stories and suggested scientific explanation, the mystery of Hebron's Ghost Light was never really solved. Even in modern times, the light is often pointed to as one of the area's enduring mysteries. Case in point, the October 28, 2007, edition of Salisbury's *Daily Times*, mentions the light in its article on local legends done for the Halloween season. The paper noted:

"The basketball sized light was often spotted by young lovers seeking privacy on the country road, as well as by other passersby."

Is the light really gone, or will it once again pop up, puzzling travelers and playing its game with officials who are confident that they can explain it away with a few simple suggestions? Time will tell, but until then, the legend lives in the ghost lore and folktales of Maryland's mysterious Eastern Shore.

Resources and Works Consulted:

Baltimore Evening Sun July 14, 1952.

Burgoyne, Mindie. Haunted Eastern Shore: Ghostly Tales from East of the Chesapeake. Haunted America/History Press, Charleston, SC. 2009.

Daily Times, Salisbury, Maryland, July 14, 1952.

Daily Times, Salisbury, Maryland, July 16, 1952.

Daily Times, Salisbury, Maryland, October 28, 2007.

Gaddis, Vincent. Mysterious Fires and Lights. David McKay Company, Inc., Philadelphia, PA. 1967.

Seeking the Strange: Uncanny Geometries & the Art of Psychogeography
By Kevin Lee Nelson

We all get a certain thrill when we visit a location associated with a strange legend. This is especially true if it's a location with on-going bizarre phenomena. This could be a certain stretch of road known for being haunted by a phantom hitchhiker, a specific patch of woods or swamp said to be the domain of a local monster, or an otherwise normal field where a UFO was said to have once visited and left an enigmatic crop circle. While visiting these sites we become highly attuned to our surroundings, and the area becomes imbued with a sense of the weird or the uncanny. A kind of enchantment takes place. An otherwise ordinary landscape is transformed in our mind's eye by the context of a legend, and we think to ourselves, *This is where "X" happened*, or *This is where "Y" sometimes happens*. It's the electrifying sensation of being at the actual spot where something inexplicable occurred that makes legend tripping so exciting — that endorphin rush one gets when suddenly odd tales seem ever so slightly more probable. You don't have to imagine the setting because *you're already right there*. It's similar to being at a famous real-world film location used in a Hollywood movie -- a strange blurring of reality and fiction. At these places one feels like a participant in the legend and part of the tale's legacy. But what if our presence at these sites is more than just folkloric tourism? What if our presence serves a hidden function -- a critical part of the secret process?

In this article I will address a number of questions: why do certain locations seem more palpably strange than others? Does it stem from our familiarity with a particular tale or unusual history? Perhaps it's due to odd and suggestive geography or architecture that unconsciously triggers our imagination. Do some locations have embedded presences that we can sense? Is it possible for our minds to actually interact with peculiar environments in subtle ways, perhaps increasing the odds of something strange occurring to us? To put it another way, do our interactions with these enchanted landscapes serve as a catalyst for triggering anomalous phenomena, or is it all in our imaginative heads?

We've all been to places that feel a bit odd or off, perhaps for no obvious reason. In the most extreme cases people immediately sense there is something wrong with a space and they usually find a reason to remove themselves quickly. I've seen it happen. It's become a bit of a horror film trope where a psychic or some other "sensitive" enters a haunted house and is immediately rebuffed or made ill by an unseen presence. However, in reality you don't need to be psychic to sense these things. I'm certainly not. Yet we can all feel when a place feels welcoming or foreboding even if we can't put our finger on exactly why.

The Geometry of the Strange

In ancient times unseen presences were widely acknowledged and believed to be unique earth spirits associated with a given location, each with its own characteristics and personalty: the *genius loci*, or spirit of a place. In classical antiquity people were generally pan-psychic, meaning they believed that all matter possessed a soul or spirit called a *daimon* (not to be confused with the latter Christian concept of *demons*). Even rocks possessed a rudimentary type of life, though far more primitive than our own. Additionally, people believed environments were not passive, and they assumed that places actively engaged with us in an energetic and even collaborative way. But how could seemingly dead matter possess life? In Plato's *Timaeus and Critias* (a series of monologues given by Critias and Timaeus written circa 380 BC), Plato describes how geometry is the process in which spirit is distributed though matter. Geometry is all around us, whether it's the architecture of a building, the shape of a snowflake or a leaf, or the tiny crystalline formations within a rock. This was the conduit in which our environment received life, and even a certain character or personality dependent on its unique geometry or assemblages of geometries. Each location was a zone of interactions between humanity and the hidden world around us.

The spirit model of the universe continued on for hundreds of years within Western culture, especially among certain Western Mystery Traditions, like Hermeticism, Kabbalah, Alchemy, and other esoteric traditions and sects that still held an enchanted worldview. Like the Ancients, they believed that all matter held an essence of spirit, and that characteristics and correspondences of matter were determined by shape and geometry which also denoted planetary association. This is often referred to as the *Doctrine of Signatures*. This worldview continued up until the Enlightenment when the spirit model was cast aside for today's materialistic model of the universe. Today's belief that we are separate from our environment simply didn't exist in earlier times. However, the old attitudes and intuitions still occasionally creep into our modern lives. Some outdoors enthusiasts today may occasionally feel a sense of the numinous while hiking in the wilds or while soaking in the beauty of a particularly picturesque landscape. They may even sense an odd presence at certain locations, but generally speaking contemporary society views the physical world as something mostly dead, or at best mindless.

In today's mostly materialistic society the spirit model of the universe has been replaced by the psychological model. This began with psychologists like Freud and Jung who theorized that much of how we view the world, and how we behave in it, is explained by psychology. In a nutshell, our perceptions of reality are all in our head. That's not to say they aren't real, but they are *subjectively* real. They are formed by our own unique neuro-programming, which is the result of biology and personal experience. Whereas the Ancients and Renaissance alchemists lived in a world of objective and concrete reality, we mostly live in a post-modern world of subjective reality where the world is defined to a degree by the observer. To make things even more confusing, if one reads the most cutting edge philosophy or the so-called "spooky science" of quantum physics, one will encounter the term *omnijective*, meaning that matter *could* be simultaneously both subjectively real *and* objectively real.

So how does psychology apply to places and spaces? Modern architects often use psychology to create different psychological effects within buildings. Famous early 20th century architect Frank Lloyd Wright frequently used his *compression and expansion* technique to manipulate the emotions and perceptions of occupants. Large airy spaces would be connected by low, dim, and cramped vestibules and corridors. As occupants move through the building's connecting spaces they are compressed, which creates unease and an unwillingness to linger. Then, upon entering into the next room—usually large, tall, and expansive, there is a feeling of relief, often translating into a "wow" effect and making the room feel more impressive. Wright would also intentionally make main entrances difficult to locate for those visiting a building for the first time. He said it was so people would be forced to walk around the building first, and presumably admire its form and design. It's intentionally psychologically manipulative, but that was par for the course with Wright.

Another early 20th century architect, writer, and occultist, Claude Bragdon, went full circle by looking back to the Ancients and their belief that matter could be imbued with life through geometry. Taking inspiration from Euclidian principals, Bragdon was obsessed with multi-dimensional forms, called tesseracts, that are 2-D representations of multi-dimensionality. He believed that geometry, when perceived correctly, could give us glimpses of higher dimensions. Most of Bragdon's buildings masterfully utilized occult geometry and the golden ratio. The Rochester Train Station in Rochester, NY, was considered Bragdon's masterpiece (sadly it was razed in 1965). It was mathematically designed around a specific musical ratio. In 1917 Bragdon invited opera singer Marie Russak Hotchener to tour the station before the grand opening. According to Bragdon, she began to sing inside the large station, and when she hit the desired harmonic pitch it had a marvelous effect "At the utterance of a certain note the entire room seemed to become a resonant chamber, reinforcing the tone with a volume of sound so great as to be almost overpowering: the walls, the ceiling, the entire building seemed to cry aloud." Hotchener replied, "There! Now your railway station has found its keynote - now it is alive!"

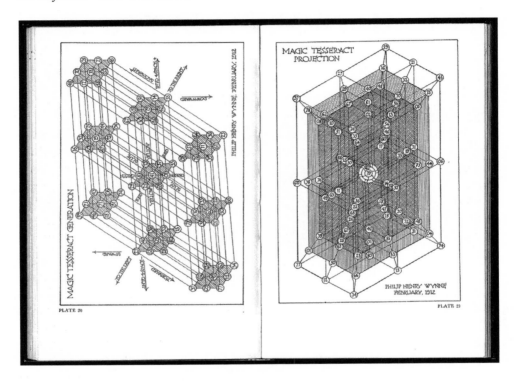

Of course, incorporating sacred geometry into architecture is nothing new. The cathedral builders were doing it during Medieval times. Cathedrals are essentially gigantic Gothic assemblages of sacred forms — a *talismanic* conglomeration of structure, ornament, and relics all in sympathetic harmony. They're essentially giant batteries of psycho-spiritual power. Everything about cathedral design has a purpose. Even something as basic as the Gothic arch is intentionally designed to draw one's eye up to a point so that people raise their faces to the heavens. I'm very familiar with this effect, as I happen to live in an 1878 Gothic Revival house designed using the Golden Ratio. It has an amazing atmosphere and an aesthetic quality that I find extremely satisfying.

I'll give you another personal example of this kind of palpable sensation. A few years ago I visited Crownthorn Chapel (constructed in 1980) in

Eureka Springs, Arkansas, designed by E. Fay Jones. It's inspired by Sainte-Chapelle, a Gothic church in Paris, France. However, instead of choosing the usual Gothic style, Jones chose the Prairie School of architecture, made famous by Frank Lloyd Wright. It's a breathtaking building — the "glass masterpiece of the Ozarks." In fact, it was named by the American Institute of Architects (AIA) as the fourth–best building of the twentieth century. As soon as I walked in, it was like entering another world. I've rarely felt such a sense of calm and tranquility. And I'm not even religious — not even a little bit. Nor do I profess to be psychic at all. It was really quite astonishing. Somehow Jones had figured out how to project an intense level of serenity through geometry. One of Jones' genius decisions was to build the non-denominational pilgrimage chapel in the woods where visitors can simultaneously enjoy the remarkable design while communing with nature directly through its massive glass windows.

While in Carlsbad Caverns I had a similarly powerful, though distinctly different, reaction to the environment. I went to Carlsbad during their slow season between Thanksgiving and Christmas — the perfect time to go. That particular afternoon I was one of the only people there other than park staff. I had practically the entire cavern to myself. When I entered the aptly named "Big Room" I was speechless. It was like being on another planet. The Big Room is the equivalent of eleven football fields long. It's 800 ft below the desert surface and the ceiling of the chamber reaches a height of 255 ft.

So here I am 800 ft deep in the earth in a room that's so high I can't even see the ceiling, it just disappears into darkness. It almost felt like I was outside on a starless night. Within the chamber are massive stalagmites that are the size of small high-rise buildings. The cave is so massive that it makes you feel incredibly tiny as you walk around megalithic rock formations and peer down seemingly bottomless chasms. I have never before seen pitch-black abysses like that. The setting reminded me of those scenes from science fiction movies where adventurers explore a hollow earth.

I was almost overwhelmed by an intense feeling of awe. My surroundings were so incredible and surreal that it felt like I was dreaming. Stranger still, I had the impression the environment was in possession of an ancient intelligence or awareness. Naturally, my thoughts went back to the beliefs of Hellenistic times and their logic rang more true than ever. The towering megaliths seemed like ancient slumbering gods. The telluric current in that underground world was unmistakable and potent — almost heady and intoxicating. It's an absolute wonder. Hours later when I finally emerged a bit stunned and blinking at the daylight I felt like I'd had some kind of visionary experience or arcane initiation.

I've also experienced the opposite response from a location. Years ago I was camping alone in a large forest owned by a friend. I'd camped there a few times before, so I was very familiar with the landscape. I had a favorite spot to set up camp that was down in a ravine near where two dry creek beds intersected. After I set up camp I decided to try to engage with the environment and test out some theories. I had the Greek concept of *daimons* in my mind, and I wondered if I could figure out a way to make a connection with the spirit of this place. The two creek beds created a sort of natural crossroads where they joined, so I figured that would be a good place to make a statement to whatever forces may exist in that valley. I built a small cairn out of rocks on the spot and asked the spirits of the valley to make their presence known. Nothing happened — at first.

Hours later, as the sun was going down, I was sitting by the fire when I slowly started to feel a slight sense of unease. I didn't think much of it at first, as I figured I was just tired or concerned about how my untested new camping equipment would hold up overnight. After finishing my dinner, I started listening to the radio and tried to relax. By this time it was good and dark, especially far back in the woods and down in the valley where I was. Gradually the feeling of unease got stronger. Whereas before it was just a minor sensation, now I had the distinct feeling of being watched. I tried to brush it off and told myself I was being silly. This was remote private land, and the likelihood of anyone being out there in the dark was slim to none. Still, the feeling persisted. Not only that, but it grew with each passing minute.

As a precaution I grabbed my tomahawk and set it across my lap, figuring it would make me feel better if nothing else. While I sat there in my camp-chair I tried to sense any movement beyond the firelight. I switched off the radio so I could better hear whatever may be out there: the snap of a stick, or the sound of a dislodged stone in the creek bed. The biggest animals in the area were deer and coyotes, but there were also rare sightings of mountain lions. Occasionally I would suddenly shine my flashlight out into the darkness trying to catch a figure or the eye-shine of some critter, the source of my increasing apprehension, but beyond the immediate campsite the beam was instantly swallowed by the night. I recall thinking how eerily quiet it was. Normally there were the typical night sounds of insects, frogs, and other nocturnal critters in the area, but on this night it was dead silent, which only heightened my apprehension.

A couple hours passed, and as much as I tried to ignore it, my sense of dread only increased. I began to have the distinct feeling that *something* didn't want me there. It was like an oppressive force emanating from the darkness. And not just from all over; it felt like it was coming from a specific direction, the direction of the creek bed. A definite presence. As bad as it was, I got the impression that it was still asking nicely. For now. I wasn't sure I wanted to be around when it *stopped* asking nicely. It made me annoyed because the relaxing night in the woods I'd envisioned clearly wasn't going to happen. I'm not a jumpy sort, or one that gets rattled very easily, so this was a very uncharacteristic reaction for me, which only made me convinced that something really unusual was happening. Unsettled and frustrated, I realized that I didn't want to spend the whole night on edge, and that if I packed up then I could still get home before 1am. So I took the hint, packed up, put out the fire, and left.

It was inexplicable. I have no idea what that was. Was something really watching me from the darkness, or was it my imagination? Did I disturb or awaken some unseen force down in that valley? Did I provoke the *daimon* of that particular valley by building the cairn? Why didn't it ever happen during the other times I camped on that very same spot? Perhaps the cairn disturbed the energetic flow by changing the geometry at the confluence of the two creek beds. It's a common belief that hauntings often occur during or after a building has been renovated or remodeled. Change seems to stir things up. Perhaps the physical change in the environment is all it took to trigger a malevolent force. I should note that one of the primary woodland spirits in Greek mythology is the god (or daimon) Pan, which is where we get our word "panic" from. I have no idea what it was, and I've never been back.

The Art of Psychogeography

Today we often use different terminologies for describing the *spirit of a place*. People of a more New Age bent use terms like "vibes"or "energy" (without being precise about what type of energy). However, when referring to a place's atmosphere, mood, aesthetics, or feeling of unseen forces or presences, the term that's the most apt and useful for me is psychogeography. The origins of the term can be traced back to Paris in the 1950s. Philosopher, filmmaker, and founding member of Situationalist International, Guy Dubord, defined *psychogeography* as, "the study of the specific effects of the geographical environment, consciously organized or not, on the emotions and behavior of individuals"; or more simplified, it is the effect of the *outer* upon the *inner*. It's where psychology and geography collide, providing a means of exploring the behavioral impact of environments.

Originally the concept of psychogeography was mostly applied to urban areas. One common technique is to lay open a large map of a city. Then randomly place a glass (or some cylindrical object) somewhere on the map. Next, trace the circumference of the glass on the map. Now you have your route. The objective is to walk this route staying as close as possible to the traced line. It forces you, the wanderer, to go places you'd typically never go, see things you wouldn't usually see, and perhaps meet people you'd otherwise never meet. The goal is to pay particular attention to your environment; notice the architecture and its function; pay attention to signs, advertisements — even graffiti; listen in on conversations of random passersby. Use your mind's eye to imagine what the street looked like a decade ago, fifty years ago, a century ago, and even before there was a city. Then you will feel like you've taken the pulse of the quarter. It's practice that requires mild concentration and a little patience. But above all it requires curiosity.

Once you "tune in" to the environment you may notice some strange patterns, coincidences, and synchronicities. Maybe even a bit of deja vu. We all know that every district and neighborhood in a city has its own distinct flavor, but the objective is to look deeper and uncover what really makes an area tick, and then open up a line of communication. Eventually, if you practice it enough you can start to pick up on subtle transmissions from your surroundings. It's a form of urban divination. You may notice messages on advertisements, or even a piece of trash, that seems meant for you or relevant to a question you had in mind. Or you may catch part of a song that has a special meaning to you or that seems overly coincidental. The idea is to turn part of a city into your own giant ouija board. Through it you can converse with whatever entities are bound to the environment, even if those entities are simply your own unconscious mind.

Years ago, my colleagues at Back Roads Lore and I made a peculiar observation. We started noticing a certain motif whenever we explored legends and strange cases. We noticed that whenever we found a clue or item of interest for the case we were researching we would also see something with a frog on it nearby. It turned up in countless ways: a bar called The Bullfrog, product packaging with a logo with a frog on it, or something more conspicuous like a big roadside fiberglass statue of a frog. It happened so often that we began to look for frogs whenever we were on a research trip — an on-going synchronicity. If we saw something with a frog on it we knew we were getting close to a mystery. It's almost like the universe is playing with us. Frogs became landmarks that something pertinent to our research topic was nearby. The rule is: if we see a frog we pull over. Why it chooses to appear in the form of a frog is anyone's guess. It's the cosmic trickster communicating in a way that is beyond our understanding.

In addition to the glass and map technique, we occasionally throw a dart at a map of a state. Then, based on where the dart lands, we go to the nearest town and spend a weekend there. Our goal is to discover whatever strange and unusual legends the area has to offer. Over the years we've discovered that every place has a tale to tell, or a number of tales. What town doesn't at least have a local haunted house?

To make it even more fun, we make a competitive game out of it. Whoever digs up the most interesting legends wins. Usually the prize is a 6-pack of beer or something similar. You never know what bizarre local lore you may find. Obviously, we start by going to the local library, historical society, and museums, but in my experience the best place to go is a local tavern. Some things never change. Usually there are a handful of older locals that are more than willing to discuss their community's folklore. Another great resource is teens. A group of teens hanging out around the local convenience store is usually a goldmine for stories. They know them all. I know I did.

I'll give you a quick example. When I was a teen there was a story about an older woman named Lillian who lived in the next town over. People said she was a witch. According to the legend, if you pulled up to her house and said, "Lillian, are you there?" she would suddenly appear in her yard and walk toward you, or even try to get in your car. It could be any time of day or night. Naturally, as teens we had to see if there was any truth to it. We found out where her house was and pulled up to it around midnight, parking on the street in front of the house without going on the property. I remember it was cold and pouring rain. The yard was overgrown with weeds and one of the trees had fallen over the driveway. The place looked nearly abandoned. One of my friends got out of the car and said, "Lillian, are you there?" softly, not enough to wake anyone up or cause a disturbance. To our shock and disbelief, just moments later an old woman walked out from behind one of the pine trees and started walking toward our car. She must have been there the whole time, even at midnight in the pouring rain. As you can imagine, we got back in the car and got out of there as fast as we could. Was she really there? Was it our imagination playing tricks on us? Were we tapping into the specific psychogeography of the location to trigger an effect? To this day I have no explanation for it.

Have you ever gone Randonauting?

A very new way to have unexpected encounters and discoveries is by "Randonauting" via the Randonautica app. It's a novel idea, a psychogeographical tool for the 21st century. According to the website, "Randonautica is a tool created to enhance the human experience with novelty by mindfully exploring the world, the interconnectivity of the universe, and to test the hypothesis that human consciousness can influence the distribution of random numbers through Mind Matter Interaction ... the Randonautica app was created to encourage people to venture outside of their day-to-day routine by using quantum random number generators to derive a truly random coordinate to a journey." I like to consider it a form of guerrilla legend-tripping.

The entire process of Randonauting and how it works is beyond the scope of this article (though I will be writing an article specifically devoted to Randonauting in a future issue of BRL), but I can give you an abbreviated explanation. Using the app, you enter in a radius from your current position. It could be just your neighborhood, or it could be miles wide — your choice. Then it creates points or zones of statistical anomalies though the use of a random number generator. Points are categorized as either an "attractor" or "void." An attractor-point is an area where quantum-points are highly concentrated far beyond a statistical average and considered significant. In contrast, a void-point is the opposite of an attractor-point where quantum-points are abnormally sparse. This can be useful, as it has a better chance of being relevant toward your intention. The goal is to discover and visit locations of statistical anomalies and see what's there. Sometimes people add an intention before the location is calculated. For example, one may add, "I want to find something red and round." Once they arrive at the site they may discover they've been led to an apple orchard, or perhaps they wind up at the sign of a Target store. You'd be surprised at how many times people encounter something that matches their intent. The creators of Randonautica admit they don't exactly know how it works, yet it seems to work for thousands of users.

Hopefully by this point you're eager to get out there, go beyond the blacktop, and have your own weird and wonderful adventures. Remember that unusual encounters can happen, but you have to get out there, and the key ingredient to make that happen is you. Be the catalyst of your own far-out forays into our strange and mysterious world.

Resources and Works Consulted:

Coverly, Merlin. *Psychogeography*. Pocket Essentials. 2006.

Ellis, Eugenia Victoria. Claude Bragdon and the *Beautiful Necessity*. RIT Cary Graphic Arts Press. 2010.

Harpur, Patrick. *Daimonic Reality.* Pine Winds Press. 2003.

Hildebrand, Grant. *The Wright Space: Pattern and Meaning in Frank Lloyd Wright's Houses*. University of Washington Press. 1991.

Lecouteaux, Claude. *Demons and Spirits of the Land*. Inner Traditions. 1995.

Legard, Phil. *Psychogeographia Ruralis*. The Lark Field Press. 2011.

Massey, Jonathan. *Crystal and Arabesque: Claude Bragdon, Ornament, and Modern Architecture*. University of Pittsburgh Press. 2009.

Nigel Pennick. *The Eldrich World*. Arcana Europa Media. 2019.

Plato. *Timaeus and Critias*. Penguin Classics. 2008.

Randonautica website. (2023). About Randonautica. https://www.randonautica.com/about

The Phantom Grave Digger of North Dakota
By Chad Lewis

Many people take pride in their goal to visit and explore all 50 states in America. Somewhere along my pursuit—I am currently stuck at 44 states---I came across some research discussing the very last state people needed to cross off their list in order to complete all 50. I was a bit surprised to find that a large percentage of people did not need to visit the most obvious far-flung states of Hawaii or Alaska, but instead they only needed to visit North Dakota to complete their plan. For whatever reasons North Dakota seems to be the forgotten state, which is odd because it sits in a straight path for those looking to head out to the wild west, or for those western travelers making their way out east. North Dakota is not like Maine where you specifically need to make it your final destination in order to see it. North Dakota makes a perfect pass-through state for those looking to venture to other more popular locations.

Personally, I really enjoy traveling through North Dakota, especially the far western portion where the landscape shifts to something resembling the landscape from another planet. My favorite North Dakota town is a quaint little western outpost called Medora. With a permanent population of just over 120 people (minus the thousands of tourists), Medora pushes right up against the entrance to the fantastically beautiful Theodore Roosevelt National Park, which also happens to be one of my favorite national parks.

In 1883, the Marquis de Mores decided that the harsh land outside of the North Dakota Badlands would make the perfect location for a new settlement. Naming the town Medora in honor of his wife, Medora von Hoffman, the Marquis quickly set up several stores, a beef processing facility, a school, a church, and several other buildings, including his own magnificent chateau. As wild and rugged as the fledgling town was, one wide-eyed easterner immediately fell in love with the remote wilderness of the area. That man, of course, was a young Theodore Roosevelt. Long before Teddy became the 26th President of the United States, he was seeking to hunt bison and experience the solitude and grandeur of the Badlands.

Besides being known for its most famous resident, the historic town of Medora is also chock-full of haunted stories and legends. The Medora Fudge and Ice Cream Depot, housed in a historic old bank building, and is thought to be haunted by the ghostly apparition of an unknown female spirit. The only catch to this legend is that the spirit will only show up on her birthday, and since no one seems to know who this might actually be, you have a 1 in 365 chance of experiencing her. Apparently, none of the previous witnesses took the time to mark down the date of their encounter. Outside of the birthday appearances, I spoke with employees of the shop who informed me that objects will often move on their own, as though shifted by some unseen force. An old, non-working antique clock positioned inside the building will sporadically chime before going silent once again. Staff members told me that they often get the sense that someone or something is in the store with them.

Originally constructed in 1884 as The Metropolitan, the Rough Riders Hotel is a beloved lodging option for travelers visiting the area. For decades, guests and staff alike have reported a smorgasbord of strange things occurring at the hotel. Whenever I stay at Rough Riders, I choose a room on the top floor due to a legend that the third floor is haunted by the wandering spirit of a young boy who will suddenly appear in front of you. Guests have frequently heard the sounds of a young kid playing loudly in the hallway outside their room, yet when they fling open the door to see what all the racket is about, the hallway is completely empty. Inside the rooms, guests report faucets turning on and off on their own, and doors that mysteriously open and close by some unseen force.

In his book *Haunted Dakotas: Ghosts and Strange Phenomena of the Peace Garden and Mount Rushmore States,* author Andy Weeks also lists the Chateau De Mores, The Billings County Courthouse Museum, and the Little Missouri Saloon as other haunted places sprinkled around this tiny town. Plus, we can't forget those who believe the spirit of Mr. Roosevelt himself continues to roam the rugged landscape that he loved so deeply. When you consider that the entirety of Medora fits within a couple of square blocks, the sheer number of known haunted locations could arguably make it the most haunted town in North Dakota.

As much as I love haunted hotels and ice cream parlors, my absolute favorite legend of Medora involves the historic cemetery that rests on the outskirts of town. Sitting atop of a small hill overlooking the town, the Medora Cemetery is a constant reminder of the pioneers and early non-indigenous settlers that battled the unforgiving weather and landscape to create this charming little town. Officially, the cemetery dates back to the 1880s, as evidenced by the grave markers of that period scattered throughout the grounds. Unofficially, the site is rumored to have several unmarked graves that pre-date any official use of the graveyard.

The cemetery is also a bit of a dichotomy, straddling both the old pioneer days, and the modern progress of Medora. For decades, a gravel road would lead you to the secluded piece of land that the graveyard occupied. It was just far enough outside of the main downtown area that it didn't cast an eerie presence over the town. This all changed in 1958 with the nearby construction of the Burning Hill Amphitheater, which houses the immensely popular and wildly entertaining Medora Musical. Every year, thousands of excited tourists drive up the long, paved road to reach the amphitheater's spacious parking lot. Most visitors are so preoccupied by their excitement for the upcoming show that they remain oblivious to the sharp gravel turn off that leads to the cemetery. It is odd because the cemetery is right down the road to the most popular destination in Medora, yet it remains all but hidden to those who are not specifically searching it out.

I first learned of the legend of the phantom gravedigger from the book *From the Pecos to the Powder: A Cowboy's Autobiography as told to Ramon F. Adams*. In a larger piece on the strange, haunted legends of the Chateau De Mores, the author threw in a section about a mysterious phantom that prowls the graveyard hill. You can see the Chateau from the graveyard as you look down the steep embankment. Since this is Medora, of course the Chateau is said to be haunted as well. The most frightening sighting at the Chateau is the spirit of a black sombrero-wearing man who, in an argument with the Marquis over water rights, found himself hunted down and killed by the Marquis' hired hands. His spirit frequently slinks itself along the shadows of the Chateau as though trying to remain undetected. Locals believe that the spirit is on a never-ending quest to locate his killers.

The justice-seeking black hatted ghost isn't the only spirit that is not resting peacefully. Dating back to the 1800s, witnesses have reported seeing the ghostly figure "of a man who would go with pick and shovel toward the little graveyard on the slope and dig in the night by lantern light." The strong, sturdy, and hearty townsfolk, the exact type who you would think wouldn't get spooked by anything "swore to the truth of this and that they had heard the rattle and pick of this ghostly digger as he made a grave there in the rocks and gravel." Imagine sleeping in the shadow of the North Dakota Badlands only to have your slumber interrupted by the clanging sounds of a ghostly pickax ringing through the town. Today, legend tells that the spirit of the gravedigger can still be seen lumbering up the steep incline leading to the cemetery. The most prevalent explanation for the ghostly behavior is that perhaps this gravedigger from beyond is preparing a grave for the return of the Marquis, who had left Medora in the autumn of 1886. Perhaps the spirit is endlessly forced to dig his own grave. A more ominous theory, and one that I personally find fascinating, points to the apparition digging the grave of whatever hapless witness is unlucky enough to catch sight of him plying his trade.

Adding more intrigue to this mystery is the fact that no one seems to know who this phantom grave digger might have been. Was he the town's old gravedigger from days gone by? In the old days, the geographical seclusion of Medora, accompanied by the brutally harsh weather conditions, made the area rife with struggle and setbacks. Surely the town would have employed a grave digger of some sort. Regardless of the spirit's true identity, the sinister nature of this legend is more than enough to cause the most seasoned legend tripper to be on high alert when visiting the cemetery. Every time I wander through the cemetery, I catch myself peering over my shoulder in search of the ghost, and although I have never made his acquaintance, I make sure to listen intently for the dreadful sounds of his pickaxe at work.

Resources and Works Consulted:

Kennon, Bob. Pecos to the Powder: A Cowboy's Autobiography as told to Ramon F. Adams. University of Oklahoma Press. 1965.

Weeks, Andy. Haunted Dakotas: Ghosts and Strange Phenomena of the Peace Garden and Mount Rushmore States: Ghosts and Strange Phenomena of the Peace Garden and Mount Rushmore States. Globe Pequot. 2023.

Sanford Florida's Headless Miser
By David Weatherly

In the late 1800s, the state of Florida was booming. The Civil War was in the past, the Reconstruction era (1865-1877) was complete, and people from all over the country were moving to the Sunshine State hoping to start anew. While some came for the warm temperatures, many were attracted to the state because of the growth of the citrus businesses. New residents snapped up citrus groves and land and set their sights on creating a prosperous trade in fruits. In short, it was a different kind of gold rush. Large tracts of land were filled with lush citrus trees. During harvest season, the groves were swarmed by work crews and pickers who plucked the fresh fruits and filled wooden crates to be shipped to points far and wide.

Among the new arrivals was an Ohio native named Sam McMillan. McMillan quickly gained a reputation as a miser. Not just a penny pincher or tight spender, but a died in the wool Dickens style miser. He didn't trust banks and refused to put his money in them. As a result, he carried around large amounts of cash stuffed in a wallet or passbook that was so fat that he had to keep it shut by tying a shoestring around it. People said that the wallet was so thick that no matter what pocket the man had it in, it was noticeable because of the bulge that it created.

Whenever he left his home for more than a day, McMillan also carried a gold watch and chain and two or three gold rings that he wrapped in a piece of buckskin and tucked in a pocket.

McMillan had moved to Florida during Reconstruction and built a successful business, but by late 1881 he'd had enough of his life as a citrus grower. Perhaps it was the climate, a big change from his native Ohio, or maybe it was the work itself; whatever the case, he was ready to sell his citrus grove and return north.

McMillan's desire to sell his business and leave Florida is what brought Archie Newton into the picture.

Archibald Newton was an Englishman from a wealthy family. He had arrived in Florida via river steamer two years before the McMillan murder.

Newton had come to the United States from London after experiencing some trouble there. Newton's story has a lot of strange elements, some of which made it easier for people to believe he had something to do with the McMillan case.

In the spring of 1880 Archie was living in a boarding house in London run by a woman named Charlotte Bowron. Charlotte had two daughters—Kate and Pollie—who helped her run the business. Trouble came when Pollie accused Archie Newton of drugging and raping her. Not only that, but Pollie also claimed that she was pregnant with Newton's child.

Not only did Newton somehow survive the scandal and legal entanglements, but he ended up married—to Pollie's sister Kate.

After his numerous trials and tribulations in London, Newton made his way to America looking for a new start in life. He set his sights on Florida and the potential for wealth in the citrus business.

When Sam McMillan started talking about selling his grove, the rumor was that Archie Newton was a potential buyer.

On September 30, 1882, Sam McMillan was seen walking to Archie Newton's home. People assumed that the two were going to talk business. It was the last day that anyone saw Sam McMillan alive.

Stereoview of Sanford, Florida in the mid-1800s

Archie Newton was seen, though. People said the man was acting strange when he was out and about on Sunday, October 1. His odd behavior reportedly included buying a bottle of wine and asking a neighbor if he could borrow a "sharp razor." He also claimed that he'd shot an alligator outside his home the night before. These claims were among the things brought up later when Newton was accused of killing his neighbor.

On October 17th, Sam McMillan's partially dismembered body was found submerged in nearby Crystal Lake. The body had been tied down with a rope and weighted with a burlap sack filled with an iron pot full of nails. The body had been in the water almost three weeks and was in terrible condition. It was decomposed and decaying, and aquatic scavengers had clearly been feasting on the remains. Most of the internal organs had been devoured, both the hands were missing and most of the appendages were barely attached, hanging on by just a few tendons. Perhaps most disturbing of all—McMillan's head was missing.

Archie and Kate Newton were both arrested on suspicion of murder and Archie was later charged with the crime. The murder case was the talk of the county and citizens discussed the whole affair in depth in the months leading up to the trial.

Although some of the evidence against Newton seemed questionable, many locals were quick to assume his guilt. After all, he was still an outsider, and an Englishman.

There was also an assumed extra brutality to the crime since many people assumed that McMillan's murderer had also decapitated him. In actuality, it was never determined how the man's head had become detached from the body, though evidence seemed to indicate that it was not due to the killer decapitating him.

The missing head was considered a vital component of the trial and officials wanted it for the inquest. The local constable ordered a renewed and more thorough search for the missing body part. When the search party directed more attention to a search of the lake, they soon found the dead man's missing head.

The head, or rather the skull, was located about twenty-five feet from the spot where the body had surfaced. The flesh was gone, and the jaw was detached, but there was little doubt that it was the head of Sam McMillan.

Understanding the importance of the skull as evidence, the men who found it jumped on the first train and made their way to the county courthouse where the trail was being held. Reportedly, the men entered the courtroom as the preliminary hearing was taking place. They walked over to a table and plopped down a sack containing the severed head.

Medical examiner Dr. F.A. Caldwell was called on to inspect the remains. During his examination he discovered a ragged hole at the base of the skull. It seems that Mr. McMillan had been shot in the head. The skull still contained brain matter which was soft and decomposed. When Dr. Caldwell shook the skull, those present heard something rattling around inside. As the startled witnesses watched, a bullet dropped out of the skull, leaving no doubt as to the cause of McMillan's death.

It was clear that while the gunshot to the skull was the cause of death, it had not caused the head to detach from the body. Officials pointed to the presence of hungry gators and snapping turtles in the water where the body was found, animals more than happy to take an easy snack tossed into the water for them.

Orange County Courthouse

With the skull as further evidence of the murder, people testified about Newton's movements and strange behavior after McMillan's disappearance. The accused man's morals were called into question; officials reported that several items belonging to Sam McMillan were found in Newton's home. It was likely no surprise when Newton was found guilty and convicted of murder. The story wasn't over, however. Newton's case was appealed to the Florida Supreme Court, and two more years of investigation and legal maneuvers unfolded. The Supreme Court ruled that much of the evidence against Newton was circumstantial. Beyond that, key testimonies were found improper and inadmissible. The court ruled that there was not enough direct evidence tying Newton to McMillan's murder. As a result, the verdict was overturned, and in December 1886 Archie Newton was acquitted of all charges in the death of Sam McMillan.

Archie and Kate Newton fled Florida and, understandably, never returned to the area.

After Sam McMillan was murdered, neighbors reported hearing terrible noises coming from his abandoned house. This was followed by the appearance of a specter in the area, a headless one that walked with a bent over stoop among the orange trees searching, it was assumed, for its missing head.

As it turned out, the gruesome phantom had been roaming the area for about a year at that point, having started right after the McMillan murder. The specter was seen within a radius of several miles of the old McMillan property and locals had no doubt whose ghost it was.

As if the headless ghost wasn't creepy enough, there was more. It seems that the ghostly head of the corpse was also floating around.

People living along Crystal Lake claimed to see a head rise from the water and float in the air above the surface of the lake. The headless corpse soon made its way to the lake and reached out with its rotting arms, trying to snatch the head from the air. Bizarrely, the head was said to flee the grasping hands of its own body and fly about the area, moaning in pain and crying out, "Why did they part us? Where's my body?"

The strange ghost story spread all over Central Florida and even out of state. An article in the November 12, 1890, edition of the *Atlanta Constitution* recounts the tale of the headless spirit under the headline "A Miser's Ghost."

According to the report, a group of five men had heard the story of the headless ghost and its floating head and decided to try to see if for themselves. The men went out to the old McMillan property and camped in the miser's abandoned house while they waited for the phantom to show up. Hours passed, midnight came, and there was still no sign of the headless ghost. The men decided to pack up and abandon the watch, but just as they prepared to leave, "an unearthly groan broke on their ears." Looking toward the sound, they saw what they had been waiting for—the headless body of Samuel McMillan was before them. It moved about, blood running down the torso from the mutilated neck. The body moved around, its posture bent and its arms searching, grasping about in search of its missing head. The weird apparition headed for the lake and the men followed, curious to witness the next part of the drama.

The men watched as the body made it to the lakeside. The *Constitution* described what happened next:

"As the horrified onlookers gazed, they were horror-struck to see a bloody head with staring eyes arise from the water and float toward the headless form. The latter seemed to see it, and rushed toward it, uttering a moaning noise. The head flew off, however, with a sound between a gurgle and a mocking laugh, and the horrible race began."

The men watched, wide eyed, as the bizarre spectacle played out. At times, the grasping hands would almost reach the floating head, but the head itself kept just out of reach, "impelled by an irresistible force, which it seemed unable to combat," the paper reported.

According to the report, "the chase was kept up for two hours." Unsuccessful in catching its own head, the body finally ran off with a roar of rage and ran back toward the old McMillan home. As for the head, it returned to the pond, landing on the water, and sinking back beneath the surface to its resting place at the lake's bottom.

The *Constitution* says that at this point, the men fled the scene, though it seems strange that they suddenly ran after watching the strange chase for two hours. The report also notes that three of the men returned to the scene the following day, but this time, they had a different mission. Reasoning that the entire haunting was due to the dead man's search for his missing body part, the group retrieved the head from the pond, dug up Sam McMillan's body in the graveyard, and reunited the two pieces in one coffin, after which he was reburied.

The news says that this process "settled the ghost" and afterwards, there were no more reports of the headless phantom or the floating head in the area. Some, of course, question the authenticity of the tale. The story in the Atlanta paper ran without a byline so it's unclear who originally penned the report.

Andrew Fink notes that this story originated from Tavares, Florida, the town founded by Alexander St. Clair Abrams in 1880. This is interesting since Abrams was the prosecutor during the murder trial. Fink writes:

"Since it references a location of the murder somewhere between Sanford and Tavares, and since Abrams himself was a former journalist not unfamiliar with sensationalism, it's probable that he wrote it" (Fink, *Murder on the Florida Frontier*).

Oddly, the story was picked up by another newspaper that same year. Sort of. The December 20, 1890, edition of Pittsburg, Pennsylvania's *Daily Post* ran a story under the headline "The Miser's Ghost Laid." The following lines of the report stated: "His Headless Trunk Had a Series of Gruesome Chases After the Head," and "The Parts Buried in Separate Graves."

The Pittsburg story repeated some of the passages of the Florida account word for word; however, the article claims that the event took place "about one mile southwest of the Mountville U.P. church in Perry Township." This would place the story in Berks County on the eastern side of Pennsylvania.

The Pittsburg article says the victim was "an old bachelor farmer, who was a miser. And as it was supposed that he had a good deal of money about his house, he was often cautioned that he would be robbed or murdered or both."

THE MISER'S GHOST LAID.

His Headless Trunk Had a Series of Gruesome Chases After the Head.

THE PARTS BURIED IN SEPARATE GRAVES.

•

And the Specter Went Away Only When One Tomb Held Both.

A SPOOK STORY FROM LAWRENCE COUNTY.

In this version of the story, the man's headless corpse was discovered under a pile of brush in his yard. The paper reports that it was some time before the head was discovered when it eventually floated to the surface of the water in a nearby pond. The paper reports:

"It was a ghastly object when first seen floating around the pond with its open eyes and hideous wounds. The body was buried in one place, and as the head was not found till long afterward and it was buried in another grave."

The Pittsburgh article goes on to recount the tale of the headless ghost and floating head, using many of the same passages as those written in the Florida article.

There's no doubt that the Florida report was the original one in this case. First of all, it predates the Pennsylvania article, and furthermore, there are no names or detailed information reported in the northern account. Overall, it seems that some lazy writer plagiarized the idea of the miser's headless ghost and passed it off as a different "news" piece and claimed

61

that it was a local event.

The story was reprinted yet again in 1893. This time it appeared in a periodical called *Romance—Being the Tales of the New York Story Club*. The story was published as "A Miser's Ghost: A Weird Tale of Life in Florida."

Why someone felt the tale fit in a publication titled "Romance" is anyone's guess. At least this version took the tale back to Florida and its original source. It is notable that the volume contained fiction by well-known writers such as Robert Louis Stevenson and Rudyard Kipling, so take that for what you will.

Author Andrew Fink brings up some important facts regarding the story that Sam's spirit was put to rest, namely, it seems that no one knows where the body was buried.

When McMillan's body was found—less its head—on October 17, 1882, it was already in a state of great decay. Edgar Harrison, the coroner, examined the remains immediately and it's likely that the rotting corpse was buried as soon as Harrison had completed his work. As for McMillan's head, it wasn't found until four days later—on October 21, but it was kept around for the trial which was held in June 1883. By that time, the head was a glistening white skull that was passed around to the jurors for examination.

Fink notes that no records have turned up to indicate where McMillan's body—or his skull—were buried. Fink writes: "For all we know, Abrams or Foster kept it as a souvenir. Or perhaps some court personnel took it home or gave it away or sold it as a relic after Archie was acquitted in 1886. Or maybe it sat in a crate of other evidence accumulated by the Orange County court, forgotten on a wooden shelf in a dusty storage room" (Fink, *Murder on the Florida Frontier*).

As the author reports, no one could have dug up the body and the head and reunited them in one coffin since there's no record of where either one ended up!

The theory that the skull may have been taken as a souvenir might seem macabre to the modern reader, but given the time period that the events occurred, it's very possible that this is exactly what happened. A fascination with the bizarre and unusual, as well as the glut of dime museums and personal collections of odd items, would have made the skull appealing, not just because it was a human skull, but also because it was the skull of a man who had been murdered and the relic of a sensational trial.

Archie and Kate Newton may, or may not, have gotten away with a horrible crime, and there are historians who fall on both sides of the argument. One thing is for sure—the murder of Sam McMillan remains an unsolved mystery. It's unlikely that we'll ever know with complete confidence who the culprit, or culprits, were.

Today, the area where Sam McMillan's property once sat is a very different place. The orange groves are long gone. Most of the pleasant, rolling hills have been leveled to make way for modern developments. Twin Lakes itself is nothing more than the name of another generic subdivision and one of the two lakes is even gone—drained out long ago to make way for another road.

Convenience stores, townhouses, shopping centers, gas stations and more fill the space. The whole area is framed by Interstate 4, its eight lanes of traffic creating a constant buzz from the vehicles racing by, headed for destinations unknown. Old Sam McMillan wouldn't even recognize the place if he saw it today.

While it is doubtful that Sam McMillan's body and head were ever reunited, the tale of the ghostly corpse faded from memory and there have been no modern accounts of any such phantom roaming the area. When I was in the area in 2020, I casually asked a few people if they'd ever heard of the Sam McMillan case or the story of the headless ghost. Out of about a dozen people, only one old timer reported that he'd heard the story of a headless ghost being in the area "in the old days." Still, one never knows when such a spirit of the past may rise again, stumbling around a modern subdivision in search of its lost head.

Resources and Works Consulted:

Atlanta Constitution, Atlanta, Georgia, November 12, 1890.

Daily Post, Pittsburg, Pennsylvania, December 20, 1890.

The Henry Shelton Sanford Memorial Library and Museum, Sanford, Florida.

The Museum of Seminole County History, Sanford, Florida.

Fink, Andrew. Murder on the Florida Frontier: The True Story Behind Sanford's Headless Miser Legend. History Press, Charleston, SC. 2018.

The New York Story Club. Romance—Being the Tales of the New York Story Club. New York Story Club, New York, NY. 1893.

Orange County Courthouse photo courtesy of the State Archives of Florida.

Ghost Town Gazetteer:
The Curse of Bodie
By Kevin Lee Nelson

For a few short years between 1877 and 1881, Bodie, California was a bustling gold rush town in the eastern Sierra Nevada Mountains about 75 miles southeast of Lake Tahoe. The town is named after W.S. Body (or Bodey), who discovered small amounts of gold in the area's hills. At its peak it had over 2,000 structures and a population of about 8,000 people, but like many boomtowns, eventually the mines went bust. In 1881 the "bust" began and slowly people began leaving Bodie, seeking fortune elsewhere. The climate in the high desert is very unforgiving, so without the lure of gold people moved on to more hospitable areas.

Unfortunately, two large fires, one in 1892 and another in 1932, reduced the town's remaining structures to only a fraction of the 2,000 buildings that once stood in Bodie. Even after the fires a few stubborn stragglers carried on until mining officially ceased in 1942. By 1950 Bodie was abandoned and nearly forgotten, and, due to its extreme remoteness, it remained untouched for decades. Ironically the geography and climate that hastened Bodie's demise (a cool and arid climate nearly 10 thousand feet above sea level) is also what kept Bodie preserved. What remains of the town is near-perfectly preserved in a state of arrested decay after total abandonment for the better part of a century. Bodie was designated as a National Historic Site and a State Historic Park in 1962.

It's an amazing experience to wander the streets of a town-sized time capsule. One really gets a sense of the past when peeking in dusty windows or walking past abandoned wooden wagons. Bodie is not a tourist trap like other old west towns such as Deadwood or Tombstone. There are no fudge shops, T-shirt stands, or dramatized reenactments. Keep in mind there are no restaurants, gas stations, or places to charge your phone. The only accommodations are restrooms at the parking lot. This is a dead town — a true ghost town. The only full-time residents are the ones buried in the local cemetery. It's the real deal Old West just as it was.

And what ghost town would be complete without eerie legends? If you visit Bodie please don't take anything as a souvenir — just leave history where it is, or you may incur the Bodie Curse. It's said that if you remove anything from the town; even a bit of broken glass or a rusted piece of metal, you will be cursed with bad luck. Your claim will run dry too. Even if the curse doesn't get you the authorities might, as it's illegal to remove anything (even rocks).

Some say Bodie is a ghost town full of real ghosts. People report apparitions and sounds of saloon brawls, but the one thing that is reported most is the "Angel of Bodie". The Angel is the ghost of a little girl who stood too close to a miner swinging a pickaxe. He accidentally struck the little girl in the head killing her. Her real name was Evelyn, and she's buried in the graveyard overlooking the town. Maybe it's a good thing the park closes at dark.

Bodie is perhaps the quintessential ghost town. I've been to countless ghost towns over the years, but Bodie comes the closest to the classic image many of us have in mind when we think of a ghost town. All it needed was for some tumbleweed to go rolling by. If you ever want an authentic sense of what the real Old West was like, you can't do better than Bodie.

Park Website: https://www.parks.ca.gov/?page_id=509

Park Address: Highway 270, Bridgeport CA 93517

Behind This Curtain:
Fouke Monster Mart
By David Weatherly

It's amazing how many fascinating and unusual stops you can find in small towns. Case in point, an outpost in Fouke, Arkansas that pays tribute to a legendary monster movie.

The movie in question is *The Legend of Boggy Creek*, and the stop in Fouke is The Monster Mart.

The inspiration and focus for Fouke's Monster Mart is a local legend, one that inspired a movie now considered a classic. *The Legend of Boggy Creek* was the directorial debut of the late Charles B. Pierce and told the story of a swamp creature said to lurk in the region's Sulphur River Bottoms. The low budget production premiered in 1972 and went on to gross more than 25 million dollars. The movie inspired generations of cryptozoologists, some of whom search for the creature to this day.

The ape-like beast is described as somewhere around seven feet in height, 300-500 pounds, and covered in dark brown or black hair. The Monster Mart's website has a perfect quote from the movie, one that captures the essence of the legend:

"If you're ever driving down in our country along about sundown, keep an eye on the dark woods as you cross the Sulphur River Bottoms... you may catch a glimpse of a huge, hairy creature watching you from the shadows" (Narrator, *The Legend of Boggy Creek*).

The Monster Mart itself is a popular local convenience store with a selection of drinks and snacks. It's also a top selling outlet for Hunt Brothers' pizza, and there are gas pumps out front so you can fuel up before your next stop. But beyond this, Fouke's Monster Mart is much more.

Photo ops abound, from the amazing monster motif on the building's exterior to the areas inside the museum portion of the shop. Items related to the area's famous monster and the film that brought it to national attention are all around. Photographs, vintage newspaper articles, maps, casts of the monster's footprints, and more.

There's a gift shop area devoted to the monster as well. T-shirts, hats, coffee mugs, stickers, books and DVDs are just some of the items on offer. If you see something you like, snatch it up, the store cycles through a lot of unique items and some of them never return.

Fouke's Monster Mart is a must-see location for fans of Bigfoot, cryptids, and classic monster movies and visitors have poured in from all fifty states and around twenty-five different countries.

The Monster Mart is located at 104 Highway 71, about fifteen miles southeast of Texarkana.

FOUKE

BOGGY CREEK

JONESVILLE

ULPHER RIVER

Did Lumberjacks Ever Encounter Bigfoot Creatures?
By Chad Lewis

In 2021, I wrote a book called *Lumberjack Creatures of the Northwoods*. This thin monograph featured 20 of the most unbelievable creatures that the lumberjacks of the 1800s and early 1900s believed lurked in the thick inexhaustible forests throughout the country. These were the most terrifying creatures that the lumberjacks could ever imagine. After an extremely long and exhausting day of cutting trees, the lumberjacks would retreat to their bunkhouse for a precious few hours before sleep overtook them. As the winds blew and the snow howled outside in the pitch-black darkness, the lumberjacks would sit in their bunks, smoke their pipes, and tell tall-tales to the greenhorns (young rookies). These fanciful yarns were meant to scare, warn, initiate, and entertain the new workers in the camps.

The big woods of the north seemed inexhaustible, a never-ending sprawl of dense forest where anything was not just possible, but probable. Think of the Jackalope, the Hodag, and the Hoop Snake to name just a few. In fact, lumber era scholars have discovered over 100 different creatures that made their way into the folklore of the lumberjack. These creatures were thought to roam all throughout the United States and Canada, from the wooded eastern areas of Vermont, Maine, and New York, to the giant western forests of Oregon, Washington, and California.

Since the publishing of the book, I have done dozens of lectures on the topic, and after each presentation someone will inevitably ask me if the lumberjacks ever encountered any Bigfoot-like creatures. This is an extremely tough question, as the answer is very nuanced. Part of the believability and allure of the strange Northwoods creatures is that they often resemble known animals. Take the Hugag for example. If you had to compare it to some common animal, the most likely comparison would be that of a moose, except the Hugag's mouth and lips are so long that they nearly touch the forest floor. Its neck and head are completely hairless and resemble sun-dried leather, while the rest of its body and tail is covered in long shaggy hair. I always like to compare it to Sesame Street's Snuffleupagus.

The Splinter Cat is another believable creature that is some sort of large cat-like beast, which, depending on its age, is somewhere between the size of a calf and a bulldog. Long spikes poke out from its back, giving it the appearance of an overgrown mutant porcupine. It has an anvil hard head which it uses to smash into hollow trees as it searches for food. The splinter cat is said to prowl at night or during heavy storms. Intense storms were common in the days of the lumberjacks and with each powerful blast of thunder or lightning, the men would blame it on the splinter cat out on a hunt. The Splinter Cat is no doubt based on all the cougars and mountain lions that freely roamed the Northwoods during those days. The formula for lumberjacks seemed to be---take a known animal, spice it up a bit, and voilà, you have a new species of mysterious creature.

But did these rough and tumble lumberjacks ever encounter any Bigfoot creatures? The answer is yes. Of course, they never described it as a "Bigfoot" as the word wasn't coined until 1958. Even the word "Sasquatch" wasn't known to them, so the lumberjacks, along with the rest of the general public, often referred to large hairy bipeds as "Wildmen" or a "Wildman of the woods." In other cases, witnesses would report seeing a humongous gorilla or ape-like creature out in the woods. A perfect example of the Wildman/Bigfoot similarities comes from the April 9, 1891, article published in the *Woodland Daily Democrat*. Outside of Ramsey, California, where a Wildman was spotted, witnesses described the animal as "being about 6 feet high when standing, which it did not do perfectly, but bent over after the manner of a bear. Its head was very much like that of a human being. The trapezius muscles were very thick and aided much in giving the animal its brutal look. The brow was low and contracted, while the eyes were deep set, giving it a wicked look. It was covered with long shaggy hair."

Whatever this Wildman beast thing was, the good people of California were unable to catch it.

Sometimes the lumberjack encounters only produced odd footprints, like the ones found at the Kaiser Lumber Company near the town of Winter, Wisconsin. In the January 7, 1908, edition of the *Eau Claire Leader*, the newspaper ran the story of lumberjacks who were "startled upon arising Monday morning to see the snow trampled down by bare feet...The tracks came from the north, circled around the sleeping shanty several times, paced back and forth to the barn and finally disappeared in a westerly direction."

Although the paper made no mention of the size of the mysterious prints, it was said that both feet were "plainly seen in the snow." Needless to say, the lumberjacks were perplexed at the idea of a bootless man wandering through the snow and ice to inspect their isolated lumber camp during the dead of winter.

Outside of what appear to be genuine encounters with Bigfoot, lumberjacks also believed in several forest monsters that seem to be heavily influenced by our traditional idea of what a Bigfoot looks like. Now, am I proposing that the following unbelievable creatures were actually Bigfoot?—no, but as you will see, some of the similar physical descriptions and behavioral characteristics between these odd forest creatures and Bigfoot make for a fun and interesting thought experiment.

1. The Hide-behind

Description—Have you ever been out on a leisurely hike through the woods when you suddenly get the uneasy feeling that someone (or something) is watching you from behind? Perhaps you spin around a time or two hoping to find another hiker on the path, only to discover that absolutely nothing is there. The farther you go, the more unshakable the feeling that you are not alone becomes. Finally, you quicken your pace as the hike quickly loses its enjoyment. It would be all too easy to chalk up your unsettling feeling to an overly creative imagination. Yet many old-timers know the real reason behind your nervousness----the Hide-Behind! As its name implies, the Hide-Behind is always hiding behind you. No matter where you go in the woods, the Hide-Behind will always be hiding behind you. If you quickly spin around 180 degrees, the Hide-Behind will still be behind you. Because of its superhuman ability to hide behind objects (trees, rocks, stumps, etc....) it is believed that no one has ever actually seen one---or at least no one has survived long enough to tell anyone of their sighting. It is said that the Hide-Behind is so skilled at hiding that it can hide behind itself. The vagueness of its physical appearance gave the lumberjack's mind free reign to conjure up the most terrifying version of the Hide-Behind.

Bigfoot Similarities – When it comes to the Hide-Behind you might be able to sense it, smell it, or even hear it, but you will never ever see it. The same could be said for some accounts of Bigfoot. One of the trademarks of modern Bigfoot sightings is the terrible smell that seems to accompany the beasts. Witnesses often notice a horrible stench in the air before/during/ or directly after encountering an unknown biped. Often described as being a rotten mix of body order, wet dog, skunk, and musk, the odor certainly leaves an indelible mark on the witnesses' olfactory senses. The Bigfoot-like creature spotted throughout the Everglades region of Florida had such a pungent odor that it eventually was dubbed the "Skunk Ape" as it looks like an ape and smells like a skunk.

The reason the Hide-Behind is so feared among lumberjacks is its ability to abduct men without leaving behind any trace of where they went. As soon as you let your guard down, the Hide-Behind will swiftly leap from its hiding space and disembowel you, before carrying you off to its lair where it can enjoy its dinner (you) in private. The *Green Bay Press* Gazette claimed it was "the most insidious creature" in the woods, and the *Casper Star Tribune* dubbed the Hide-Behind as "the most maddening menace in the forest." Perhaps the most cautionary account of the beast came from The *Bradenton Herald* which wrote that the Hide-Behind was a "dangerous animal believed to be the reason a number of lumberjacks turned up missing."

Let's take a look at that last sentence from the *Bradenton Herald* where they claimed "a number of lumberjacks turned up missing." If you have been following recent trends in the Bigfoot research community, you will undoubtedly be familiar with the controversial *Missing 411* series of books. The books highlight a troubling number of cases where people inexplicably go missing from the woods, often in national parks. The belief that Bigfoot creatures are behind these enigmatic disappearances and deaths has grown exponentially over the last decade or so, igniting a contentious debate as to whether or not these disappearances are supernatural in nature. It is not my goal to jump into that debate in this article, I am merely pointing out the similarities of people going missing in the woods 200 years ago. Back then, it was blamed on this fictional lumberjack creature rather than a hairy bipedal predator.

2. The Tote-Road Shagamaw

Description—The Tote-Road Shagamaw is perhaps the most bizarre and puzzling creature of the Northwoods. Even the most seasoned hikers, hunters, and lumberjacks are unable to explain its odd behavior. Early hunters often discovered the prints of what appeared to be a bear roaming the big woods. Excited at the thrill of the chase, the hunters would follow the prints for a while when all of a sudden, the tracks changed to the distinctive hooves of a moose. Old timers suggested that perhaps a moose had befriended a bear and they were wandering the woods together, yet this explanation still could not account for the fact that only one set of tracks was found, even if those tracks represented two separate animals. In 1921, *The Daily Times* reported that the Shagamaw's "shoulders are like those of buffalo," and that "the rough hair of the shoulders gives way to a soft monkey fur in the middle of the back." In 1924, the *Pawnee Courier* described the Shagamaw as a "cross between a gorilla and a lion." The *Pittsburg Sun* described its odd head as being "a cross between a cow and an ape."

Bigfoot Similarities – If you are familiar with Joshua Cutchin and Timothy Renner's two volume set *Where the Footprints End: High Strangeness and the Bigfoot Phenomenon*, then you are well aware that sometimes Bigfoot encounters make absolutely no sense at all. Similar to how the Tote-Road Shagamaw's prints inexplicably change, disappear, and are generally confounding, much of the same can be said for some Bigfoot prints. Often prints will strangely start or end in the middle of a field with no obvious origin or end point. Giant footprints will lead down a path or trail only to puzzlingly disappear. There is no doubt that lumberjacks came across a wide variety of animal tracks while working in the forest. While moose, bear, elk, bobcat, deer and others might have been easy to identify, what would they do with tracks that bore no resemblance to any of the fauna of the region? Perhaps, this is when the Tote-Road Shagamaw was born.

3. The Agropelter

Description—In appearance, the Agropelter resembles a lanky ape-like being. It has a slender hairy body with disproportionately long arms. Its ape-like face is permanently locked in anger. It loves to lurk in hollowed out logs and on the top of hollowed out trees. When an oblivious hiker or lumberman passed by, the monster would swing out its long arm and hit the person with a thick tree branch. The attack was executed with such brutal force that practically no one survived the attack. Most people exploring the forest tend to set their eyes to the ground in order to avoid tripping and falling; the Agropelter, high up in the tree, was all but invisible to any wandering lumberjack or hiker. In a 1924 article, the *Kansas Star* warned that the Agropelter "is a tough customer and no woodsman hankers to meet one." The *Longview Daily News* wrote that "many a lumberjack has been killed by a dead branch aimed by the deadly accurate Agropelter." Making matters worse, the Agropelter is thought to be an expert stick thrower, which allows it to attack from a much further distance.

Bigfoot Similarities – In the last 10 to 20 years, one of the most popularized portions of Bigfoot folklore is the creature's alleged penchant to throw objects at people. Although its weapon of choice tends to be rocks and stones, nearly any imaginable object will do the trick. Heck, back in 1969, Texas' Lake Worth Monster even chucked a car tire at some witnesses.

In the summer of 1988, Bob Reiman found himself staring at a giant red-eyed, white-furred Bigfoot-looking creature standing in the darkness a few miles outside of Murphysboro, IL, in the junkyard that Bob owned. Bob and his security guard slowly backtracked to the safety of the old beat-up garage. As the two men tried to plot their escape, the monster could still be heard lurking about outside in the pitch-black darkness. A few seconds later, the men were startled by a loud bang on the door. The noise sounded as though something heavy was thrown up against the door. Soon another blast came from the side of the building, followed by several others, each intensifying in sound. Bob believed that the creature was simply taunting him by tossing rocks and boulders at them, as he firmly believed the beast could have easily smashed through the door if it had wanted to.

With all the prosperity and convenience associated with the lumber days, we tend to overlook the devastating impact that clear cutting the forests had on the environment. If we view things from the perspective of the inhabitants of the forest, we begin to see how the never-ending encroachment of humans and the swift and dreadful destruction of the woods could leave the creatures with a sour taste in their mouths. None of these creatures were more resentful of humans than the vindictive and deadly Agropelter, whose hatred for humans was unmatched in the big woods. Could we make the same argument when it comes to Bigfoot? If these Bigfoot creatures are flesh and blood animals that truly live among the last hidden portions of our country, would they too not be pissed off a bit by the continued loss of their habitat? From this viewpoint, all of the tossing and throwing of objects would serve as a warning that this land is occupied, and that you should stay out.

When it comes to Bigfoot chucking things at people, these above-mentioned stories are just the tip of the iceberg, or more aptly—the tip of the tree limb. Perhaps the old school lumberjacks also had everything but the kitchen sink tossed at them, and in order to make sense of the odd occurrences, the Agropelter was born.

4. The Whirling Whimpus

Description—Let's start with the physical descriptions that come from eyewitnesses who have spotted the beast and somehow miraculously survived to tell their tale. The Whimpus stands around seven feet tall and has a long muscular gorilla-like body that is covered in a light fur. Attached to the imposing body are two tiny hind legs, but the creature's front legs (or arms) are what you should be afraid of. In his book, *Fearsome Creatures*, Henry Tryon described the beast's front legs as being "disproportionately long, sinewy and powerful." As threatening and intimidating as the Whimpus looks, its ghastly actions are infinitely more terrifying.

The Whimpus is a super carnivore, an apex predator, and a non-picky one at that. It will eagerly devour bears, deer, hogs, turkeys, lumberjacks, lost hikers, hunters, or whatever other poor soul crosses its deadly path. Its favorite means of hunting is to stealthily stand near a bend in the road and wait for any unsuspecting lone travelers to wander along. When its prospective meal gets close, the Whimpus stretches out its long burly arms and begins to rapidly whirl around on its pointy hind feet like a spinning top. As it spins faster and faster, the Whimpus reaches such incredible rates of rotation that it becomes practically invisible.

Bigfoot Similarities – At over 7 feet in height, just the sheer size of the Whirling Whimpus quickly eliminates the possibility of its being nothing more than a misidentified forest animal. This becomes even more evident when you throw in its heavily muscled gorilla-like body that is covered in a thick dark matted-down fur. Those astute students of folklore will also be quick to point out that the Whimpus' disproportionately long arms match up nicely with the physical descriptions normally associated with Bigfoot. Outside of the obvious physical likenesses to Bigfoot, what intrigues me the most about the Whimpus is its ability to move so fast that it becomes virtually invisible.

If you look outside of the general stereotypical accounts of Bigfoot sightings, you will discover many instances where the Bigfoot creatures look as if they are moving at impossible speeds. As bizarre as it may seem, I have spoken with several witnesses who are convinced that the creature they spotted moved considerably faster than any known animal on this planet. I am including one such puzzling story from my 2011 book, The *Wisconsin Road Guide to Mysterious Creatures*. The case involved a woman named Loretta who lived with her family on secluded reservation land. Over the course of several months the family was plagued by a series of baffling and terrifying Bigfoot encounters. On one occasion Loretta spotted a Bigfoot creature peering into her daughter's bedroom window. This caused her grave concerns because at the time, her daughter was having a birthday sleepover and her room was filled with her friends. Here is what happened next:

Loretta moved in for a closer look and was shocked to discover a large, thin, hairy beast lurking outside the window. Loretta described the creature as being around 7-8 feet and noticed that its body was covered in matted down hair. Strangely, the image reminded her of one of the apes from Tim Burton's *Planet of the Apes* movie, except that the being's hairless grayish face appeared eerily human. At this point Loretta's olfactory sense was overwhelmed from a strong odor that she could only compare to rotting onions. Perhaps sensing Loretta's fear, the creature darted away from the house at such a speed that Loretta claimed that she could barely see his movement.

Does the creation of these lumberjack creatures provide proof that lumberjacks encountered Bigfoot-like creatures, long before the creatures came into public awareness?---absolutely not. However, they provide a keen insight into the thoughts and beliefs of those who were living and working in the very same environments where sightings occur today. Historical journals and newspaper articles allow some measure of understanding as to what these men were encountering. The real drawback of using these accounts as definitive proof is that we have to approach any lumberjack sighting with a grain of salt. On the one hand, it certainly appears as though they had encounters with Bigfoot creatures, yet by the same token they also told stories of the fur bearing trout and an assortment of highly laughable animals. So where does this leave us when it comes to lumberjack sightings? For me, these fantastical stories are meant to remind us that we do not have all the answers and that weirdness is all around us, especially in the most remote and wild places of the forests.

Resources and Works Consulted:

Bradenton Herald. April 16, 1986.

Casper Star Tribune. December 5, 1982.

Cutchin, Joshua & Renner, Timothy. *Where the Footprints End: High Strangeness and the Bigfoot Phenomenon*, Volume I: Folklore. Independently Published. 2020.

Cox, William. *Fearsome Creatures of the Lumberwoods*. Judd &Detweiler. 1910.

Daily Times. August 18, 1921.

Eau Claire Leader. January 7, 1908.

Green Bay Press Gazette. February 25, 1973.

Kansas City Star. May 2, 1924.

Lewis, Chad. *Lumberjack Creatures of the Northwoods*. On the Road Publications. 2021.

Lewis, Chad. *The Wisconsin Road Guide to Mysterious Creatures*. On the Road Publications. 2011.

Lewis, Chad & Nelson, Kevin Lee & Voss, Noah. *The Big Muddy Monster: Legends, Sightings, and Other Strange Encounters*. On The Road Publications. 2019.

Longview Daily News. February 13, 1965.

Longview Daily News. February 18, 1965.

Pittsburg Sun. August 30, 1921.

Pawnee Courier Dispatch. May 15, 1924.

Woodland Daily Democrat. April 9. 1891.

Figment or Foopengerkle?
The Legend of Sinkhole Sam
By Kevin Lee Nelson

When people think of North American lake monsters, they usually think of Lake Champlain's "Champ" in upstate New York, or perhaps "Ogopogo" of Okanagan Lake in British Columbia. Folks from the upper Midwest might be aware of stories of "Pepie" from Lake Pepin between Minnesota and Wisconsin where the Mississippi River widens into a lake the size of Loch Ness. There are many dozens of famous lake monster stories, and nearly all of them originate from the northern portion of the continent. There's a reason for that: *because that's where most of the lakes are.* However, there are always exceptions. Even though the Great Plains of Kansas might seem like one of the least suitable habitats for a lake monster, that's exactly where "Sinkhole Sam" calls home.

It sounds far-fetched (and let's be honest, it certainly is) but there's a certain logic to some of the tongue-in-cheek explanations for how a giant worm-like creature could turn up in the plains of Kansas. For example, the Arapaho tribe, which has lived in Kansas since at least the 17th century, after European expansion pushed them out of the Minnesota region, has legends of a large horned water serpent called the *Hiincebiit* (pronounced heen-chabb-eet, meaning "water master" or "owner of waters" in Arapaho) that lived in the area's lakes and rivers. They believed that these dangerous and powerful water monsters were mostly benevolent as long as people paid them the proper respect. Sometimes the *Hiincebiit* would even reward people who gave them offerings by granting them good luck in hunting or war. As for those who didn't pay the proper respect; well, you know how that story usually goes....

Prior to the 1920's there used to be a string of small freshwater lakes in the area north of Wichita, KS. These were mostly drained for farmland, leaving only two remaining bodies of water. The larger of the two is Lake Inman, just to the west of Inman, KS. It's roughly one hundred and sixty acres and is the largest natural lake in Kansas. The other is Big Sinkhole (that's its official name according to the Kansas State Department of Transportation), just three miles south of Lake Inman as the crow flies. It's at Big Sinkhole where the Sinkhole Sam story began. It's much smaller than Lake Inman, and its size fluctuates greatly depending on drought conditions. It was roughly one hundred acres and fifteen feet deep in 1952 when the Sinkhole Sam story first made headlines.

The Legend

Though some claim that stories of a large serpent in the Inman area go as far back as to the 1920s, the legend really took off in 1952 when two unidentified fishermen reported seeing something very strange in the Big Sinkhole. It had been a dry year and water levels at Big Sinkhole were lower than normal, making it easier to spot whatever lurked in its waters. What they saw was a large worm-like creature roughly fifteen feet long and the diameter of an automobile tire. Shortly after, Albert Neufeld and George Regier were fishing off the bank of Big Sinkhole when they saw the creature. Neufeld had presumably heard the stories, as he had taken his rifle along as a precaution. When he saw the creature rise out of the water he fired a couple shots at it. They went back into town with their story, and it caused a huge stir in the community. Neufeld stated that he thought he killed it. However, his companion Regier was doubtful. From where Regier stood the shots didn't seem to have much effect.

Soon after, carloads of people were lining up along 10th Avenue where it hooks around Big Sinkhole. The owner of the land, Mil Penner, described in his book *Section 27: A Century on a Family Farm* how he came home from church one Sunday to see dozens of cars parked along Big Sinkhole. Everyone was hoping to catch a glimpse of the strange creature that by this time had been dubbed Sinkhole Sam. I suppose Sam could be short for either Samuel or Samantha. According to reports, many so-called "responsible witnesses" observed Sam, and most generally agreed that it was worm-like, about fifteen feet long, roughly twenty-one inches in diameter, had a flat head, and a "non-snakelike" mouth. Most generally agreed that it looked like a gigantic worm or eel.

How did it get there?

Naturally, people wondered how the creature got there. Everyone seemed to have their own theory. Some residents theorized that perhaps the area's sinkholes were connected to vast subterranean caverns deep underground, and the sinkholes were just tiny surface gateways to the hidden watery realm. It would explain how such a large creature could survive and grow to enormous size in such a seemingly small space. Additionally, it would also explain why there were some stories of Sinkhole Sam popping up in Lake Inman three miles away.

Another hypothesis was that the creature was a relic from the earlier larger lake system, and it was marooned there after the lakes began to shrink and disappear. Without any competition for food or risk from natural predators it grew to an abnormal size. Others thought that it had been flushed into the sinkhole from the nearby Little Arkansas River, as the area was prone to flooding.

One popular theory placed blame on the oil-drilling operations of the 1930s. They speculated the creature was some kind of undiscovered worm from deep in the earth, and the drilling had disturbed a hidden ancient ecosystem full of monster-sized organisms. If this sounds like the plot to a Godzilla movie, keep in mind the first Godzilla movie came out just over a year later in 1954. People wondered if the oil company's drilling had given Sam a pathway to the surface by wiggling up through one of their core drill holes, eventually finding his way to the sinkhole.

What was Sinkhole Sam?

People in the Inman area had a lot of theories. One of the leading theories was that it was a very large eel. Eels in Kansas are extremely rare, but they do turn up occasionally. In 2015 an angler caught a 30-inch American eel in the Kansas River below the Bowersock Dam outside Lawrence, KS. That eel was *very* far from home. How far? American eels spawn in the Sargasso Sea of the Atlantic Ocean. Department of Wildlife, Parks and Tourism Fisheries section chief, Doug Nygren, stated, "This eel made a long journey from the Atlantic Ocean, through the Gulf of Mexico, up the Mississippi, took a turn at St. Louis to enter the Missouri River, and another turn to go up the Kansas River to the Bowersock Dam." That's a heck of a journey, but it had time. American eels can live up to 20 years. The current Kansas state record for an American eel is one caught in 1987 (also from the Kansas River) that weighed 4.4 pounds. While this is nowhere near fifteen feet long, freaks of nature do happen. Or perhaps the size of Sam was a bit of an exaggeration.

Was Sam just a big snake? Some people thought so. The longest snake indigenous to Kansas is the gopher snake, which can reach up to about ninety inches, but that's only half the size Sam was reported to be. Today people would assume it was an escaped pet, like a python, as exotic pets are far more common and popular now. However, an escaped exotic pet, like a python, would have been extremely unlikely in early 1950s Kansas. Interestingly, according to the Guinness Book of World Records the largest snake in captivity currently lives in Kansas. Her name is Medusa, and she's a twenty-five-foot-long reticulated python weighing over three-hundred pounds — even longer than Sam was reported to be. Medusa is on display at Edge of Hell haunted house attraction in Kansas City and lives on a diet of rabbits, hogs, and deer.

Misidentification of a large eel or snake (albeit a very large one) is one of the most probable explanations. There were definitely some large critters in the area. Stories going back to 1902 tell of swimmers that were afraid to go into Lake Inman because a large turtle "the size of a claw-foot tub" had made the lake its home. This account is similar to the famous "Beast of Busco," a five-hundred+ pound snapping turtle alleged to live in a farmer's pond near Churubusco, Indiana, back in 1948, and also the fabled giant turtle of "The Devil's Inkwell," a sinkhole outside of Roswell, New Mexico. Lake Inman is also known for yielding sixty-pound catfish, so the area is known for some gargantuan wildlife.

Others thought that it was some kind of unknown surviving prehistoric creature that lived deep underground — a true monster. The idea may seem laughable (and truly it is), but sixty to eighty million years ago, when what is now Kansas was a warm inland sea, the area was teeming with Mosasaurs, which looked exactly like the sea-serpents adorning old maritime maps. Mosasaurs were apex predators with snakelike bodies the size of a bus. In a 1908 article from the *Topeka Daily Capital* a Professor Willitson states that the greater Salina area (about fifteen miles north of Inman) is "full clear up to the brim of skeletons of sea-serpents." The area is a bona fide graveyard of monsters. Perhaps as the ancient seas slowly dried up, some of the descendants of the Mosasaurs found refuge in deep subterranean caverns and exit to this day, or at least until the 1950s. And if you really want to get into ultra-fringe theories, perhaps Sinkhole Sam was a phantom of the very distant past, or some sort of time slip. That would explain why bullets didn't affect it and how it vanished just as mysteriously as it appeared.

Of course, the obvious option is that the whole thing could have been a hoax. But with the number of "responsible witnesses" and "people whose veracity would not normally be called into question" claiming they saw something big splashing around in Big Sinkhole, a hoax seems unlikely. Nor has anyone ever come forward and confessed to hoaxing the whole thing, and after over seventy years probably no one ever will. Still, one article written in the *Witchita Eagle* sixteen years after the sightings hints that a local tavern owner, appropriately named Wiley Case, made the story up. It says that Wiley gave directions to an inquiring fisherman to the Big Sinkhole area but warned him of a "huge snake that lived in the vicinity," The man happened to be a reporter, and he probed Wiley for more details. Shortly after, a newspaper article was published about the creature in Big Sinkhole. The unknown reporter's name is not given in the article, but if true, there's a good chance it was veteran Kansas newspaper columnist Ernest Alva Dewey.

In the Wake of the Monster

Whether Ernest Alva Dewey was tipped off by Wiley Case or not, the excitement around Inman caught his attention. Dewey was known for writing satirical pieces for the *The Hutchinson News-Herald* where he would often poke fun at folktales and stories of alleged strange encounters. Prior to his newspaper career Dewey had been a publicity writer for a circus. Presumably this is where he developed his dramatic and sarcastic style and an appetite for the strange and unusual.

While covering a local story about a mysterious UFO sighting, Dewey attributed the phenomenon to a fanciful Kansas cryptid known as the "ball-tailed snickelhoopus," which looks like a cross between a lizard and a kangaroo with a spiked ball at the end of its tail. Not kidding. Dewey was inspired by the far-fetched yarns of the Ozarks, particularly the book, *We Always Lie to Strangers: Tall Tales from the Ozarks* by famed Ozark folklorist Vance Randolph who mentions a creature called the "hickelsnoopus." Playing upon the whimsical names, Dewey wrote, "The term "hickelsnoopus" is a perversion, or hillbillyism, for the snickel-hoopus or, as it is more familiarly known in Kansas, the Ball Tailed Snickelhoopus." He lampoons the legend further by adding, "This species is not abundant, even in Kansas, and has probably died out in Arkansas as there appears to have occurred a sort of migration from there during prohibition. Specimens frequently are reported in the sand hills of the Arkansas Valley and the smokiest of the Smoky Hills. It can be seen most distinctly through a glass, preferably about three-fourths full."

Dewey's humorous coverage of the Sinkhole Sam story was no different. His satirical article "Monster Turns Out to be a Plain Old Foopengerkle" appeared in the *Salina Journal* on Sunday, November 23, 1953. The article is absolutely dripping with his trademark sarcasm and snark and is accompanied by an illustration of a young man being grabbed and pulled off a small bridge by a large serpent with the caption, "WATCH OUT — he may forget he's a vegetarian." Dewey adopts his usual faux-scholarly persona, only this time he's accompanied by the fictitious ophiologist Dr. Erasmus P. Quattlebaum. After allegedly looking at evidence found at Big Sinkhole and interviewing witnesses, Dewey declares that the creature is an extinct "Foopengerkle," one of Dewey's whimsical and imaginary creations. The article goes on to explain why the Foopengerkle went extinct. According to Dewey it was due to loneliness, as there are only male Foopengerkles. He ends the article with a cheeky political quip, "There remains the problem of what to do about this extraneous monster. My advice is: nothing. Now that the country has gone Republican maybe he will go away." Even though the article was a comical spoof piece to give locals a playful jab, one wonders if Dewey actually checked out Big Sinkhole. It's very likely, considering he lived only about 25 minutes away in Hutchinson, KS.

Another Sam Sighting?

In the mid-1960s, stories began circulating about a giant snake spotted around Kingman, KS, roughly 35 miles southwest of Inman. In one of the stories a farmer claimed a twenty-foot serpent grabbed one of his young calves, dragged it down into Kingman County Lake, and devoured it. The creature was described by a number of residents as dark, ranging from ten to twenty feet long, and as thick as a man's body. Kingman rancher, Bill Millford, claimed he was out chasing cattle when his horse was tripped by the creature. An unidentified trucker claimed he stopped his truck when he saw a massive snake slithering across the road. It was so big that he was afraid to drive over it because it might wreck his truck.

DR. N. E. ALLISON
. . . Led the quest . . .

On August 10th, 1969, a monster hunt was organized to hunt down the so-called "State Lake Snake" or "Creature from the Kingman Swamps." An estimated whopping seven-hundred and fifty people showed up, including fifty men on horseback, to look for the elusive beast. Every motel in town was booked up. The hunt was led by Kingman dentist, Dr. N. E. "Spike" Allison, who wore a bright red pith helmet boldly lettered with "Chief Snake Hunter." Former Kansas Senator Marvin Cox served as a referee for the hunt and shouted out the main ground rule: "Bring 'em back alive!" They were afraid the swamps would turn into a war zone, so guns were not allowed; only pole snares and nets could be used. By the end of the day, they managed to wrangle up three garter snakes, one red spotted water snake, and a raccoon. It seems the Creature from the Kingman Swamps escaped the dragnet. So, either Sam has some relatives, or he really gets around — perhaps traveling along those supposed networks of underwater caverns deep under the Kansas plains.

WATCH OUT — He may forget he's a vegetarian.

Science Set Back Years

Monster Turns Out To Be A Plain Old Foopengerkle

The Legend Lives On

What was Sinkhole Sam? Is he still there? So much time has passed that we'll never know what those Kansans saw writhing around in Big Sinkhole, yet the legend lives on. I've been to the area multiple times. Lake Inman isn't very big, and Big Sinkhole is practically just a swampy puddle during dry years. But while the idea of a fifteen-foot worm-serpent in Kansas may seem like a stretch, it's at least a little more plausible than Oklahoma's freshwater octopus or Indiana's oil squids.

With the recent pop-culture fascination with cryptids, particularly among young people, the seventy-year-old story of Sinkhole Sam has fortunately been rescued from obscurity and taken on a life of its own in recent years. A number of recent online articles about Sam have appeared. One can also stream various podcasts and YouTube videos entirely devoted to the legend. Perhaps the biggest sign that Sam has hit the big time is his inclusion in a popular new collectible card game MetaZoo. Now Sinkhole Sam has his very own collectible card, part of the vast bestiary of MetaZoo. Even kids living far from Kansas will be familiar with Sinkhole Sam.

In the past, most towns were reluctant to discuss their local monster legends out of fear of ridicule, but attitudes have definitely changed, and now monsters are something to be celebrated and a source of local pride. Additionally, states and communities are waking up to the fact that monster tourism is a big industry. The annual Mothman Festival in Point Pleasant, WV, draws over twenty thousand people each year. Perhaps if the Sinkhole Sam legend continues to rise in popularity it will only be a matter of time until Inman, KS, celebrates its first annual "Sinkhole Sam Festival."

Resources and Works Consulted:

Alberty, Michael. (2020, July 10). Is There A Mysterious Monster Lurking In a Kansas Sinkhole? Kansas City. https://kansascitymag.com/news/only-in-kc/is-there-a-mysterious-monster-lurking-in-a-kansas-sinkhole/

Coleman, Loren & Huyguhe, Patrick. The Field Guide to Lake Monsters, Sea Serpents, and other Mysterious Denizens of the Deep. Tarcher/Penguin. 2003.

Native Languages of the Americas website. (2020). Native American Legends: Hiintcabiit. https://www.native-languages.org/hiintcabiit.htm

Dewey, Ernest. "Monster Turns Out to be a Plain Old Foopengerkle." *The Salina Journal*. November 23, 1952.

Dewey, Ernest. "Ozarkians Lie Awake Nights Thinking Up New Whoppers." The Salina Journal. May 31, 1951.

Flynn, Mary Kay. "Sighted Sinkhole Sam, the Monster of Kansas, But Couldn't Sink Same". *The Owensboro Messenger*. October 30, 1953.

Gilliland, Stephen. (2024, January 7). Exploring Kansas Outdoors: The Legend of Sink Hole Sam. Hays Post. https://hayspost.com/posts/d4789a92-8085-43e6-b3eb-dc35cc451ec4

Keating, Connor. (2021, October 26). Time to scream: the legend of "Sinkhole Sam." The Hutchinson Collegian. http://hutchcollegian.com/2021/10/26/time-to-scream-the-legend-of-sinkhole-sam/

Kansas Department of Wildlife and Parks. (2015, October 22). Kansas Angler Discovers Rare Eel on End of Line. https://ksoutdoors.com/KDWP-Info/News/News-Archive/2015-Weekly-News/10-22-15/Kansas-Angler-Discovers-Rare-Eel-on-End-of-Line

Katy, Dartford. (2012, September 21). The world's longest snake living in captivity... and it's kept in a haunted house! *The Daily Mail*. https://www.dailymail.co.uk/news/article-2206693/The-worlds-longest-snake-living-captivity-weighs-300lbs-25ft-long-lives-haunted-house-Kansas.html

Morrow, Darrell. "Monster Snake Eludes Hunters West of Kingman." The Wichita Eagle. August 11, 1969.

Shelly, David. "Wall Shows Inman's Past; Citizens See Bright Future." *The Mennonite Weekly Review*. June 25, 1987.

The Topeka Daily Capital. "Many Hundreds of Sea-Serpents. Western Kansas is Full of Them." April 10, 1908.

The Wichita Eagle. "Creature From Kingman Swamps: Hunt on for Giant Snake." August 1, 1969.

Penner, Mil. *Section 27: A Century on a Family Farm*. University Press of Kansas. 2002.

Welcome to Moonville
By Chad Lewis

As more and more of us move from family farms and the rural countryside to live in towns and cities, our perspective about the importance of land begins to shift and transform. In bigger cities, land is a precious commodity, it's expensive and highly sought after. Relatively new buildings are dispassionately torn down for the sake of progress and the never-ending quest for even more modern structures. Little by little, the idea that a town could simply be abandoned and left for nature to reclaim it seems a bit preposterous. This is exactly the reason that deserted places like Moonville continue to fascinate us with their endless mysteries. The appeal of these ghost towns acts like the siren's song, magically calling out to us to come just a little bit closer. In the case of Moonville, Ohio, not only is it abandoned and nearly forgotten, it is a ghost town that happens to be filled with ghosts.

When it comes to legends on my radar, Moonville is an absolute newcomer. In the fall of 2023, Kevin Lee Nelson and I were traveling from our home state of Wisconsin to Point Pleasant, West Virginia, where we were both scheduled to give presentations at the infamous Mothman Festival –a festival celebrating the region's long history of encountering strange flying humanoid-like figures. However, Kevin and I do not travel in a manner that most people are familiar with. While the majority of travelers map out the quickest route possible, Kevin and I like to meander along the nooks and crannies of the back roads. While the interstate system is quite effective in getting you from one place to another rather quickly, it certainly lacks in providing any sense of where you are actually passing through. As you travel down the main highways and interstates at 70 miles per hour, it is nearly impossible to stumble onto roadside attractions, regional history, folklore, or local customs. Our trip had already been productive as we had stopped at numerous haunted locations, a few sites where bizarre creatures had been sighted, and a couple of junk-art roadside attractions.

As we neared West Virginia, we fueled up at an old backwoods Ohio gas station. It is our common practice while making any pitstop to inquire with the locals about any must hit legends or folklore. I have found that asking around about any local weirdness at gas stations, restaurants, bars, etc...can produce remarkable stories, and help to uncover folklore that may be deeply unknown outside the region. Unfortunately, this was not one of those occasions due to the fact that the two clerks were new to the area. Plus, it was pretty evident that they had no interest whatsoever in these types of legends. However, not all was lost.

As we exited the old timey store, we paused to read the various flyers tacked up on the community bulletin board. Among all for sale and help wanted posters was a curious looking flyer advertising some sort of odd, haunted event at a place called Moonville. If it is not already apparent, this ad was like giving catnip to a cat---we were immediately hooked. With the help of GPS and some gazetteers, we mapped out a route to the vanished city and quickly headed off in search of the old mining town that no longer was inhabited. Each backroad that we followed seemed to transport us further and further from civilization. After 40 minutes of zigzagging our way up steep gravel roads out in the middle of nowhere, we felt that we had to be getting close. We were passing through the heart of the Zaleski State Forest where the sheer cliffs running alongside the road had no guard rails or protection of any kind. Kevin and I speculated about how many people lost their lives when they foolishly took the turn too fast and careened over the cliff. Eventually we pulled into a makeshift parking lot leading to Moonville, and let me tell you, when I first laid eyes on the graffiti covered tunnel, the sight was worth every minute that it took us to get there.

In 1856, Samuel Coe granted the Marietta and Cincinnati Railroad permission to construct a railroad line that would pass right through his property. In those days, wherever the railroad went, opportunity and jobs followed. Soon, an assortment of miners and railroad workers flocked to the area. Legend tells that those residents noted how the light from a full moon beautifully projected on the old train tunnel, so the settlement was named Moonville. A school and depot quickly sprung up, as did a series of dwellings interspersed throughout the wooded region.

Over the years, as the mines continued to close, residents fled the town in search of a better life someplace else. According to the Ohio Department of Natural Resources, the last remaining inhabitants of Moonville abandoned their home in 1947. Railroad companies continued to use the tracks in 1985, yet the traffic was nowhere near like the old days when Moonville was thriving. Today the land is owned by Vinton County, and upkeep comes from the Moonville Rail Trail Association. Now, all that is left of the once vibrant town is the magnificent tunnel, an old cemetery, and the nearly imperceptible foundational remains of several old homesteads.

Excitedly, Kevin and I exited our car and stood gaping at the gigantic train tunnel that had been cut through the landscape. The thick carved block letters of Moonville were highlighted by a ton of spray paint graffiti. Over the last 30 years of travel, I had seen too many train tunnels, trestles, and overpasses to even count, yet the Moonville Tunnel was hands down the coolest one I had ever cast my eyes upon. Remarkably, the tunnel stood apart from most other haunted locations which are often covered in spray-painted depictions of a penis or littered with blatantly racist and sexist comments. By comparison, the inside of the Moonville Tunnel was covered with works of art. It was evident that a lot of people visited this lonely reminder of Ohio's past. Most people make the trek out there for the same reason Kevin and I did, the ghosts!

The first written account that I could find of anything odd happening in Moonville came from an article in the *Chillocothe Gazette's* January 23, 1905, paper that claimed "The ghost of Moonville, after an absence of one year, has returned and is again at its old pranks haunting the B. & O. S.W. freight trains and their crew." Around 8:50 pm a train passing through Moonville noticed an odd sight up ahead. Standing on the edge of the tracks was a ghost "attired in a pure white robe" that seemed to be carrying a lantern in its hand. The train conductor and engineer must have gotten a fairly good look at it because they gave this colorful description, "It had a white flowing beard, its eyes glistened like balls of fire, and surrounding it was a halo of twinkling stars."

As the train got closer, the mysterious lantern swung wildly across the track forcing the concerned engineer to sound the whistle and begin to stop the train. As the train was grinding to a halt "his ghostship stepped off the track and disappeared amidst the rocks nearby." After reading this part of the encounter, my first thought was that perhaps this brightly lit spirit was simply attempting to avert a disaster by alerting the engineer about some possible danger that lay ahead. Apparently, I was not far off in my assessment, since the paper went on to state that this was not the first encounter with the lantern-wielding spirit as "it has been at this business off and on, since the collision at that point, in which Engineer Lawhead lost his life and Engineer Wash Walters was injured."

From this point on, sightings continued to occur, and Moonville quickly gained the reputation of being a haunted area. On October 24, 1978, the *Sidney Daily News* ran a Halloween season story about haunted state parks in the region. For Moonville, the newspaper included a nice spin of the original legend telling "Each night a railroad man would stand along the tracks with his lantern to signal the train. One morning the man was found lying bloodless along the tracks. There were no clues to his death." Similar to a Hollywood horror movie, this spirit likes to make its appearance on dark and foggy nights when you can spot the ghostly lantern bobbing along the train tracks.

In 1986, the lantern-carrying-ghost story took another slight detour from the original version, which is not uncommon in the field of folklore and the supernatural. For some, this re-telling of the legend would only decrease the credulity of the original legend; however, in folklore, legends rarely remain stagnant; they routinely morph and progress as each new generation incorporates its own beliefs and values into the narrative. I tend to think of it as a decade's long version of the telephone game we all played in grade school. For its October 26th article, *The Chillocothe Gazette* included a version of the legend where the train's conductor and engineer were such bitter enemies that a local man witnessed "the engineer ask the conductor to check something under the front of the train." Once the conductor was squarely positioned under the train, the engineer gave the order to pull out, thus separating the conductor's head from his body. Since that fateful evening "some people have seen the ghost of the conductor carrying his red and green lanterns along the tracks." Interestingly, the article also claimed that in addition to the ghostly lantern, you can also hear the conductor's blood curdling scream echo through the area.

On Christmas day in 2022 the *Columbus Dispatch* mentioned another layer of the legend with its article by Ceili Doyle. The article described "the piercing whistle of a train rounding a curve, the smell of lavender wafting from a woman in an old-fashioned dress." The legend of "Lavender Lady" as she is often referred to dates back to the early days of Moonville. It is said that the young woman was walking along the tracks, somehow oblivious to the sound of the train barreling toward her; she met her end in a gruesome manner. She must have been wearing a lovely perfume on the day of her demise, because unsuspecting visitors often catch the heavy scent of lavender emanating from her death site. Interestingly, the outwardly smell of lavender is attached to numerous spectral sightings across America. In my home state of Wisconsin, we have the story of Lavender Lilly, who is said to roam the backroads in a wide stretch of land spanning a couple of different towns. In St. Louis, the infamous Lemp Mansion is said to have a Lavender Lady haunting the historic home.

At the height of Moonville's population, it is estimated that around 100 people lived and worked in the area. Whether they worked in the nearby mines, for the railroad, or at any other business, life in the area was a grueling grind. To help offset this, numerous saloons were scattered throughout the region. These saloons play a significant role in the haunted stories of Moonville because it is said that more than a few unlucky souls met their demise when their drunken walk home crossed paths with a speeding locomotive.

Today, the spirits of these unknown people can still be seen staggering along the tracks at the sites where the train ended their party. These spirits are often described exactly as you might imagine---dressed in bib overalls, covered in soot, or decked out in dirty work clothes. One of the best sources of Moonville's history and hauntings is the website-- moonvilletunnel.net. The site features one such barroom brawler called "The Bully." Apparently, this unnamed town bully was a terrible person, picking on those smaller than him, cussing out anyone within earshot, and being a nasty drunk. One night the bully was forcefully removed from a local saloon and never made it home. Several days later, some locals discovered his lifeless body. Although the cause of death was never given, the rumor among the townsfolk was that someone finally got sick and tired of being bullied and put an end to it. Those who now pass through the tunnel are treated to a glimpse of his bullying when his spirit tosses pebbles and small rocks at them.

As I previously mentioned, when Kevin and I first visited Moonville it wasn't a preplanned journey, we just stumbled across the legend as though fate had predestined our visit. At the time, we had no prior knowledge of its history or ghost legends. The first thing I said when approaching the tunnel and seeing the name Moonville was that I really hoped that the residents that once lived there called themselves "Moonies." Alas, my optimistic wish has not come to fruition, as I have found no such mention of any Moonies.

Today, visiting Moonville serves as a rite of passage for those throughout the area, especially for younger folks who use Moonville as a test of bravery to see who can enter the tunnel on their own. The long list of paranormal activity experienced at Moonville continues to grow year after year. From strange floating balls of lights, fearsome apparitions, and disembodied voices, the forgotten town of Moonville has everything a curious legend tripper could ask for. If you decide to visit this remarkable little patch of land, just make sure that the spirits of the Moonies do not get you.

Resources and Works Consulted:

Chillocothe Gazette. January 23, 1905.

Chillocothe Gazette, October 26. 1986.

Columbus Dispatch. December 25, 2022.

Ohio Department of Natural Resources. https://ohiodnr.gov/go-and-do/plan-a-visit/find-a-property/moonville-tunnel.

Sidney Daily News. October 24, 1978.

www.moonvilletunnel.net.

Lost Ships of the Anza Borrego
By David Weatherly

The Anza Borrego Desert State Park is located within southern California's Colorado Desert. At 585,930 acres, the sprawling site is the largest state park in California.

There are many fascinating tales from the region: stories of lost mines, hauntings, UFO sightings, and much more. One of the most intriguing legends involves a pair of lost ships that were abandoned in the region long ago. The tale of the desert ships has so many elements that it almost makes one's head spin—Native American legends and petroglyphs, lost treasure, ghosts, and more are all wrapped up in the lore involving the ships. This fascinating hodgepodge blends history, both factual and unverified, folklore and a few dashes of the supernatural and it's not a simple story. The various twists and turns seem to shift at random as if blown by desert winds.

Could a Spanish ship really have gotten stuck in the California desert? Many experts dismiss the legend and claim that there are no primary source documents that confirm a ship's being abandoned in the desert. Sightings of the ship, they say, are nothing more than people experiencing a desert mirage induced by the blazing sun and lack of water.

Still, some researchers believe that the ship could have gotten stuck after a flood connected the Salton Sea to the Gulf of California. The connection allowed a ship to travel far inland but the water quickly receded and the vessel got stuck and was unable to return to the ocean.

The area certainly has potential to be hit with massive flooding and it would have been plausible for a ship to travel inland as the legend claims. Tidal bores have also been known to strike the area in the past and sweeping waves moving inland could have carried the galleon to what is now nothing but desert.

A large part of what makes the legend intriguing is the number of stories told by native Americans, travelers, and frontiersmen over the years. Many of the stories are brief reports of one of the ships being sighted, but other tales offer more tidbits of information and direct testimony about the lost ships. Case in point, a story from 1915. That year, in a small town in southern

California, a native of the Yuma tribe walked into a local store and gathered some items for purchase. When the man went to the counter to check out, he didn't pay with coins, rather, he pulled out some shiny pearls for trade. Locals were intrigued and began a conversation with the native man asking him where he'd gotten the pearls. The man told an odd story—he revealed that he'd spent the night in the desert in a strangely shaped house made of wood. The house was partially buried in the sand.

Several locals wanted to know exactly where the structure was, and they offered the man a deal—they would pay him several hundred dollars and give him a place to sleep for the night—if he would guide them to the wooden house the following morning. The man readily agreed. He collected his money and turned in for the night at his assigned lodging.

The next morning, anxious locals turned up ready to set out into the desert with the native man but when they went to his room, they found that he had vanished. He was never seen again.

Why were the men so eager to follow an unknown native man out into the desert to find a weird wooden house in the sand? In short, they believed that the native had stumbled on a mysterious lost Spanish Galleon that was purportedly buried in the desert.

Tales of the ship began circulating throughout southern California in the 1800s, but the origins of the ship reportedly dated back to the 1600s. Specifically, the origins of the ship are most often attributed to an expedition for pearls launched by the Spanish in the 1600s.

In 1610, King Phillip III of Spain ordered Captain Alvarez de Cordone to undertake a search for pearls on the western coast of Mexico. Cordone hired two other captains to accompany him on the expedition—Juan de Iturbe and Pedro de Rosales. He also hired forty pearl divers.

Three ships were built in Mexico and the journey got underway in July 1612. When the ships reached their destination, they began the search for pearls, stopping periodically so the divers could search the ocean floor and retrieve baskets of oysters. The going was slow and eventually the expedition came across a native village. When the Spaniards stopped and met with the villagers, they discovered that the natives had baskets full of pearls lying around. The Spanish told the natives they wanted to make a trade, offering European clothing for pearls. The natives agreed, but when the trade was made, the village discovered that the Spanish had cheated them, handing over nothing but old rags and taking the pearls that they wanted. The angered natives retaliated and attacked the Spanish.

The Spanish escaped but Captain Cordone was hit by an arrow. He survived the wound, but he fell ill and had to turn around and sail back to Spanish territory in Mexico. He ordered the other two captains to head for the Gulf of California and continue the search for pearls.

While sailing up the Gulf, something happened to Captain Rosales's ship. Some versions of the tale say it was lost in a storm, others claim it struck a reef and had to be abandoned.

Iturbe had the only ship left to continue the search for pearls. The lone galleon eventually sailed up the Colorado River and into the Salton Sea. By some accounts, the Colorado River and the Salton Sea were flooded at the time causing the water levels to be much higher. Something happened at this point in the journey—by some accounts there was an earthquake—and when the ship tried to turn around and head back out to the ocean, they discovered that their route had been closed off. Not only were they unable to access the ocean, but the water level was now dropping rapidly and soon the ship was stranded in the sand.

Stuck miles from the ocean, and unable to sail, the Spaniards had no choice but to abandon the ship and trek out of the area on foot. They took what supplies they could carry that were necessary for survival and headed west back toward the coast. Four months later, survivors of the expedition were finally picked up.

As for the abandoned ship, it remained buried in the sand and over time it sank further into the desert. The water never returned, and the blowing winds covered the old ship with more desert sand. At times, portions of the vessel were revealed, and people caught glimpses of it sticking out of the desert floor.

Travelers began to tell stories of seeing the Spanish ship in the 1800s. It's important to note here that many of the stories call the ship a Spanish Galleon. This alone has caused many historians to scoff at the legend. Galleons were massive ships, heavy and sitting deep in the water; it's unlikely that a galleon could have sailed up the river, even if the waterway was flooded.

If there's any truth to the legend, it's likely that the ship was a caravel—a much smaller vessel that had a greater degree of maneuverability. Caravels had square sails, shallow drafts, and rows of oars on each side that made them easy to move even in shallow water.

The explorer Colonel Albert S. Evans traveled through the region in the mid-1800s. Evans was traveling to San Bernardino when he entered a valley that he described as "the grim and silent ghost of a dead sea." Evans reported that the moonlight illuminated the wreck of a large ship, one that he thought must have sunk centuries before when the region was covered with water.

Also in the mid-19th century, a Cahuilla chief named Cabazon talked about a tribal legend from his people. The story was the legend of a great white bird that had sailed from far away. This is often pointed to as a reference to a Spanish ship, its massive white sails being portrayed as the wings of a great bird gliding on the water.

In the aftermath of the American Civil War, many people headed into California looking for a new start in life. Travelers crossing the Borrego sometimes reported seeing what they said was a multi-masted Spanish Galleon in the desert.

There were several reports about the lost ship in 1870. That year, several Native Americans said they'd seen the ship. They claimed it was around thirty miles west of Dos Palmas and forty miles from what was then the San Bernardino Yuma Road.

According to a report in an August 1870 edition of the *Los Angeles Daily*

News, the ship was half-buried in a drying alkali marsh west of Dos Palmas forty miles north of Yuma, Arizona. The ship could be seen from a good distance across the desert.

In 1870, a man named Charley Clusker claimed that he'd located the vessel. Clusker was organizing expeditions to travel out to the ship which was purportedly fifty miles or so from Dos Palmas in a region of boiling mud springs.

The *Los Angeles Star* picked up on the story and ran articles about the search in both its November 12 and December 1 editions but there was never any indication that Clusker had been successful in his endeavors.

Somewhere along the way, likely the early 1900s, a story circulated about an old timer in southern California who said he'd stumbled on the ship while he was out in the desert. The man claimed that he'd camped inside the rotting hull for several days. The man said that at the time, he was unaware of the legend and the treasure trove of pearls buried in the ship's hold below him. The man was never able to relocate the vessel, so the mystery remained, and his story was unverified.

In 1905, a prospector named Butcherknife said that he had found the ship buried in the sand dunes near Borrego Springs. Butcherknife claimed that the ship was fossilized.

A farmhand named Elmer Carver told an odd story involving the ship in 1907. Carver was working on the Niles Jacobsen farm near Imperial, California, about fifteen miles north of the US-Mexico border. Carver became curious about some oddly shaped fence posts on the property and asked Jacobsen's wife where they'd come from. She told him that a bad windstorm had blown a lot of sand from the dunes near the back of the couple's home. When the winds died down, the Jacobsens saw what looked like a boat sticking up out of the ground. The farmer investigated, digging through the sand and down to the wreck where he discovered a small chest full of gemstones. When he tried to pull the chest up out of the sand, it fell apart. Jacobsen used a sifter and retrieved the jewels out of the sand. He carried the gems to Los Angels where he sold them.

In 1964, Carver did an interview and told the story of Jacobsen's discovery and his own sighting of the wood fence posts retrieved from a shipwreck in the desert. The audio recording is now in the hands of a private collector.

Another search for the ship was launched in 1949 by a trio of students from the University of California in Los Angeles. The men became intrigued by the legend after discovering old newspaper accounts and they decided to set out in search of it and its potential treasure.

Armed with a 1910 Irrigation District map and stories they had collected from Cahuilla tribal members, the men launched their search. The *Los Angeles Times* reported on the expedition but like other missions to find the wreck, it apparently failed.

As one would expect, over the years, numerous variations of the lost Spanish ship arose. One variation claims that the ship was in Lake Cahuilla (in the area that later became today's Salton Sea). In this version of the tale, the Spanish ship was attacked by a band of Cahuilla Indians who lived on the lake. The natives killed the entire crew and looted the ship of food, clothing, and other items, but they were unable to break into the heavy iron chests in the ship's hold. A storm came up and the ship broke anchor, drifting away before it overturned and sank beneath the water. By the time the lake dried up, the ship had been buried deep in the sand and silt, but dry conditions and blowing winds sometimes revealed the wreck.

Some claimed that the ship was a pirate vessel—specifically the *Content*—that was captained by Thomas Cavendish. The ship was purportedly loaded with gold doubloons that had been plundered from the Spanish and was lost after Cavendish sailed it up the Colorado River.

Another tale connected the ship to a lost, warlike tribe that lived in the Indian Ocean, while yet another claimed the vessel was one of King Solomon's fleet and it had been carrying the ten lost tribes from Israel. One version even speculated that the ship in the desert was the Biblical Noah's Ark!

Not every story was completely wild. One account claimed that the "ship" was a 21-foot single mast skiff that had been mounted on wheels and used for transport across the hard desert floor. The vessel was purportedly built in 1862 by several men trying to speed up their trek across the Borrego. They reached a low point in the desert and were forced to abandon the ship. The vessel was eventually covered by sand but shifting winds sometimes reveal its location.

A guide to California, published by the Works Progress Administration during the Great Depression, mentions the tale of the Spanish ship in its entry on Kane Springs. The publication gives yet another theory to explain the legend:

"One of the most prevalent of local myths concerns a Spanish galleon that sailed into the northernmost arm of the prehistoric Gulf of California, to be abandoned there with its fabulous cargo of gold. As the sea dried up, the hapless ship sank beneath the shifting dunes...The probable inspiration for the legend was a boat built in 1862 by a Colorado River mining company, transported part way across the desert by ox team, and then abandoned because of the difficulty of the journey from San Gorgonio Pass to the Colorado River" (retrieved from *Newsweek* online February 10, 2017).

It's important to note, however, that there are stories of the lost ship that predate supposed explanations from the late 1800s.

The 1933 book, *Journey of the Flame*, written by Walter Nordhoff under the pen name Antonio de Fierro Blanco, is one of the most often quoted resources of the pearl ship story. The book tells the story of a young mule driver named Tiburcio Manquerna who reportedly came across the lost ship while working as a driver for Juan Baptista de Anza who was searching for a land route from Sonora to Alta, California.

Tiburcio reportedly went into the ship and even down into the hold where he saw some of the legendary pearls. Like many others, the man was never able to relocate the site where he had seen the galleon, though he apparently took all or part of the pearls with him when he left the ship's hold.

The Tiburcio story is significant since the events he described occurred around 1774, making it one of the earliest sightings of the lost ship in the desert.

The Vikings Cometh

As if the mystery of the Spanish ship isn't strange enough, the desert is purportedly home to another abandoned vessel—this one a Viking ship.

In 1933, Myrtle Botts, a librarian from the small town of Julian, was out hiking in the Anza Borrego Desert with her husband. It was early March, and the couple were close to the Mexican border enjoying the region's wildflowers.

One morning, the couple had a visitor show up at their camp, an old prospector who had a strange story to tell—he'd seen a ship in the desert—a Viking ship. The wooden vessel was lodged in the rocky face of Canebrake Canyon and its prow was a large, carved serpentine figure. The man also reported seeing impressions on the ship's flank where shields had been attached. It was the classic description of a Viking craft, but what was it doing in the desert in southern California?

Intrigued by the story, Botts and her husband hiked over to see the spot that the man had indicated and gazed up at the rocks. Just as the old prospector had said, there was an ancient vessel lodged in the canyon's rocks.

Because of the rugged terrain and conditions, the Bottses weren't prepared to hike all the way up to the ship to get a better look at it so they went home, vowing to return the following day to get closer to the vessel.

Unfortunately, their return trip didn't happen. Several hours after they learned about the ship, there was a 6.4 magnitude earthquake in the ocean just off Huntington Beach. The quake was strong enough to have an effect in the desert and Botts later said that the tremors shook loose rocks in the canyon that buried the Viking vessel.

Legend says that Botts wrote down the directions to the ship as the prospector had related them to her. These directions were purportedly among Botts's papers that were later donated to the Julian Pioneer Museum, but the museum itself claims that it's not in possession of anything from Botts that talks about a Viking ship.

Some have tried to dismiss the Botts account as a fabrication, but it wasn't the last time someone talked about seeing the Viking ship.

The January 1939 issue of *Desert Magazine* ran a story about the Anza Borrego's lost ships and brought up an interesting account related to the Viking vessel.

Writer Charles C. Niehuis reported an encounter he'd had with a man named Jim Tucker in Prescott, Arizona. Tucker's wife, a Mexican woman, had been previously married to a man named Santiago. Santiago claimed that he'd seen a strange ship in the desert in a narrow box canyon north of the US-Mexican border. He described the ship as "a boat of ancient appearance—an open boat but big, with round metal disks on its sides."

Before he could explore the ship further, his companions pulled him away from the area and he never returned to the spot. The date of Santiago's sighting wasn't listed, but it clearly predated the Botts account.

Could Vikings really have landed in southern California? While modern historians dismiss the idea, some people speculate that a group of Norsemen could have sailed through the Northwest passage, down the coast of Canada, around Baja, California, and then up the Colorado River. In an earlier age, the river would have allowed access to the ancient Lake Cahuilla that once existed in California's modern-day Coachella Valley.

Skeptics claim there's no evidence that Vikings ever landed on the west coast of America, nor are there any documents that indicate such a journey. The story, "experts" say, is nothing more than a tall tale. But before writing off such a possibility, it's important to note that there's some intriguing lore from Native Americans in the region that indicate that Vikings may indeed have made such a trip.

The 1939 book *The Last of the Seris*, by Dane and Mary Coolidge, discusses the native people of Tiburon Island in the Gulf of California. The authors included passages about light haired giants who were "worshiped like gods" when they came among the tribe.

The giants were dubbed "Ahnt-tay ah hek'-tahm," or, "Came From Afar Men." Some tribal members said the foreigners were yellow-haired while others said their hair was white. The book notes: "The Came From Afar Men [were] strange whalers who cooked whale meat in an enormous iron pot, ate it, and drank the oil."

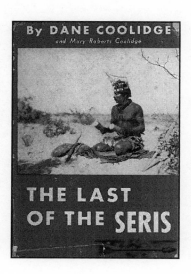

The book also reports that the giants had: "white hair and [they] were so big it took two fanegas (bushels) of tobacco to fill their pipes. They came in a big ship, in which they lived all the time, and went out in boats to kill whales. When they speared one, a man would pick it up and put it on the ship."

The story goes on to recount that the men wore big hats and drank a liquor that they would not sell or give to others. "They were very happy when they were drinking," the story says.

There was one woman with the foreigners—the wife of the captain. Her skin was even lighter than the men's and her hair was red and long and worn in braids that hung down her back.

The white giants also told the Seri that there were "many more like them in their country," where they lived in "big houses by the sea."

According to the Seri tale, the giants stayed among the tribe for "a year and four months." When they left, they took four families from the Seri tribe with them. They promised to return, but there's no indication that they did.

Author Dane Coolidge

The Coolidges believed that the tribal legend involved Norsemen who had made the journey to America's West Coast. "It is a record of the old Norsemen who visited the west cost of Mexico long before the Spanish came," they write, going on to speculate that the white men were likely Norwegians.

The book also mentions similar legends from the Mayo Nation. According to Mayo tribal lore, some of their people had rescued survivors from a strange ship that had sunk off the coast. The survivors stayed with the tribe, marrying into it over time. This is purportedly the reason why even today members of the Mayo are sometimes born with blonde hair and blue eyes.

According to the Coolidges, there are three portions of the Mayo wedding ceremony that are identical to Norwegian wedding customs.

Author David Weatherly at the Salton Sea.

Ghostly Reports

By some accounts, the lost galleon has become a classic ghost ship and people have claimed to see it "sailing" in the desert. It's said that the haunted ship emerges from the sand, its sails whipped by the desert winds. Bleached white from the blazing sun, the ship glides over the dry landscape casting an eerie glowing light. On board, dead sailors sing as the vessel moves through ghostly but unseen waters making its way for ports unknown.

Some claim this ghost ship can be seen around sunset; others say it manifests at night under bright moonlight.

Still other accounts claim that the ghost ship appears around Kane Springs where it moves in silence, gliding silently into the distance without any captain or crew in sight.

In 1878, three German prospectors said they had seen the ship at sundown about 120 miles northwest of Yuma and 40 miles east of India. The ship was floating over the desert, moving like a cloud toward the sunset.

One of the prospectors chased the ship, running off into the desert in pursuit of it and disappearing. A search party later found the man, lying naked in the sand, dead from dehydration.

The two surviving prospectors later said that the ship they had seen was massive and under full sail as it moved through the sky.

Modern Discoveries

In 2009, Robert Marcos wrote an article for the *San Diego Reader* (June 3 edition) revealing the story of some fascinating petroglyphs in Pinto Canyon, images that appear to show a Spanish ship.

Marcos was hiking with a Sierra Club group when a fellow hiker, 75-year-old Frank Johnson, dropped the news about the petroglyphs on him. Marcos got enough information about the location to make his own way to the site, a small canyon between the Jacumba Mountains and the Yuma Desert. The remote spot is close to the Mexican border and proved to be in a rugged, difficult to access area. The region is rife with dangerous natural hazards, as well as the physical risk of coming across drug runners and coyotes (human traffickers) that use the area for their illegal activities.

In fact, a border patrol agent named Ramirez told Marcos that Pinto Canyon was "a dangerous area, more of a war zone than a hiking destination," and advised him to stay away from the area. Still, Marcos was determined to see the petroglyphs and he and a hiking partner ended up making their way to the spot. Marcos described the ancient drawings:

"There were three flat rocks covered with crude drawings right at eye level. The marks had been made by scratching the top layer of rock off, revealing a lighter colored layer underneath. The drawings were stick figures of men, rectangular grids, and most notably, a tall sailing ship complete with a mast and furled sail" (*San Diego Reader*, June 3, 2009).

Marcos claims that the petroglyphs are about six miles from the purported location where Juan de Iturbe's ship went down and mentions that there are accounts from people who've reported seeing the ancient wreck. He writes:

"Most of the people who've seen the remains of Iturbe's ship were riding in off-road vehicles. One of them, Imperial Valley resident Ed Barff, provided me with a precise location. He says the caravel lies three hundred feet southeast of the eastern-most edge of the Superstition Mountains. Much of that area is designated for off-road vehicle use. But the ship's remains are located in a section reserved as a bombing range under the jurisdiction of Naval Air Facility El Centro" (*San Diego Reader* April 16, 2014).

After Marcos revealed the story of the petroglyphs, a team of experts, including historians and archeologists from the Maritime Museum of San Diego, set out to examine the site.

One expert later stated that while there's no way to be sure what expedition the ships were involved with, they certainly could have been from the early Spanish search for pearls:

"If the objects in the petroglyphs are indeed Spanish ships from one of the earlier expeditions, then it constitutes the earliest primary source graphic representation of a historic event in American history" (*San Diego Reader*, April 16, 2014).

The site is now in protected land and is not accessible by the public; however, there is a replica of the petroglyph on display at the Maritime Museum in San Diego.

Over the decades since the story surfaced, many people have trekked into the desert in hopes of finding the treasure trove of pearls, but to date, none have ever returned with solid evidence of the ship.

A modern search for lost ships in the region is problematic. The greater portion of the Salton Sink is submerged under the Salton Sea and much of the surrounding land is under U.S. military control. Some of it has been used as a bombing range and is off limits to the public.

As Robert Marcos discovered during his hikes into the area, the region is rife with dangers and is, at the least, extremely risky to travel across.

Are there really lost ships out there in the Anza Borrego Desert or are the tales simply folklore or exaggerated stories from the distant past? Maybe someday the sands will blow in just the right direction and a majestic relic from ages long ago will be revealed on the desert floor.

Resources and Works Consulted:

Blanco, Antonio de Fierro. The Journey of the Flame. Houghton Mifflin Co., Boston, MA. 1933.

Coolidge, Dane and Coolidge, Mary. The Last of the Seris: The Aboriginal Indians of King Bay, Sonora, Mexico. E.P. Dutton & Co., Inc, New York, NY. 1939.

Desert Magazine, January 1939.

Los Angeles Daily News, Los Angeles, California, August 1870.

Los Angeles Star, Los Angeles, California, November 12, 1870.

Los Angeles Star, Los Angeles, California, December 1, 1870.

Newsweek, online edition, February 10, 2017.

San Diego Reader, San Diego, California, June 3, 2009.

San Diego Reader, San Diego, California, April 16, 2014.

The San Diego Maritime Museum. San Diego, California.

Lost Ships of the Anza Borrego By David Weatherly

The Wog: Guardian of Nodoroc
By Kevin Lee Nelson

What if I told you there used to be a volcano roughly twenty miles east of Atlanta near Winder, GA, that spewed molten hot mud and flames. What if I also told you this volcano was believed by the Creek tribe to be a gateway to hell, and that it was guarded by a giant demon-dog with a forked tongue called the "Wog." Would you believe me? It gets weirder. Local legends also state that the Creek tribe used to execute their worst criminals by throwing them into the boiling muck to appease the Wog. When I first heard this tale I was skeptical too; it seemed WAY too far-fetched, like something recently made up on the Internet. But I assure you, this is an actual legend going back well over a hundred years. It's a story that has been told and retold for generations and remains an important part of Jackson and Barrow County lore.

Nodoroc

The best way to start this story is by describing the area itself. Back in the late 1700s there was a dangerous and thermally active bog called Nodoroc a couple miles east of Jug Tavern, what would later become Winder, GA. The word Nodoroc is a bit of a mystery. Early accounts state that it was a Creek word that loosely translated at "Gateway to Hell," though perhaps a better translation would be "Gateway to the Underworld," as the Creek didn't have a concept of the Christian Hell. However, more recently the traditional definition has been questioned by linguists who point out that Nodoroc doesn't seem like a Creek word, considering they didn't use the letter "r" at all. They have pointed out that "nodoroc" is a Late Medieval Dutch word meaning "swamp smoking". In fact, there was a colony of Dutch-speaking Sephardic Jews in the Jackson-Barrow-Gwinnett County area during the 1600s and early 1700s, so it's very possible the word originated with them.

That fits, because that's exactly what Nodoroc was, a smoking swamp. Early accounts say that the swamp was an extremely treacherous place with boiling blue-black mud, sinkholes, and noxious gases. The main feature of Nodoroc was a large conical mud volcano that spewed hot mud and smoke. Some early accounts mention that the place frequently burned with eerie blue flames. It's entirely possible that lightning strikes could have ignited methane gases trapped within the bog causing it to burn. The sight of strange blue flames dancing across the surface of a vast bog — like a lake of fire — would certainly be an eerie experience. In his book The *Early History of Jackson County, Georgia* G. J. N. Wilson gives an account of an early European settler named Josiah Strong and his terrified reaction to seeing Nodoroc for the first time. Strong described Nodoroc as being roughly five acres of smoking, bubbling, bluish mud about the consistency of molasses. At its center was the mud volcano that rose a few feet above the surface. He stated, "I am utterly unable to describe the scene or express in words the feeling it produces. When I take into consideration the associations connected with it and with the other more awful one described in the word of God, I am so overcome with the comparison suggested that I can only think of St. John's words in Revelation — 'And the smoke of their torment ascendeth up for ever and ever.'"

By 1784 most of the land around Nodoroc, comprising parts of today's Barrow and Jackson counties, was sold to white settlers by Chief Umausauga for fifteen pounds of beads. It's suggested in historical reports the tribe was happy to offload the land, as they perceived it as cursed and a place of devils. Because of this sale, the region was often called "Beadland." But that wasn't the end of Nodoroc. The mysterious morass still held some surprises.

In the early 1800s Nodoroc and some adjacent land was purchased by John Gossett who cleared less swampy portions for farming. One morning John noticed an unusual amount of fog hanging over Nodoroc (though it was probably smoke). As the morning wore on the "fog" did not dissipate with the rising sun, in fact, it seemed to grow *more* dense. Later, around 9 am, Mrs. Gossett saw a huge plume of smoke rise from the bog. Concerned, she summoned her husband, who was out plowing, to come and take a look. They heard a loud rumbling noise, like distant thunder — loud enough to spook their horses. Then, all at once, the entire surface of the bog shot up into the air with such explosive force that it briefly darkened the sun. Moments later, hot mud came showering down around them, spattering the Gossetts and their farm with blue-black Nodoroc muck. Presumably the sudden eruption was caused by a buildup of methane beneath the peat bog.

After that, Nodoroc seemed to settle down. Area residents said it was the New Madrid earthquakes of 1818-1819 that finally put an end to the thermal activity in Nodoroc. The earthquakes are estimated to have been between 7.2-8.2 in magnitude, which would have definitely been felt by residents of Winder, GA. Later, the dormant morass was fenced off because farmers were losing too many cattle after they'd wander off into the quagmire. Eventually the land became the property of John L. Harris (1849-1933) who decided to drain most of the swamp for additional farmland. While plowing, Harris would frequently unearth bones and horns of animals that had perished in Nodoroc over hundreds of years. One wonders if any of these were Pleistocene megafauna that fell into the pits thousands of years ago.

According to the accounts of early settlers the Creek tribe had a stone altar at Nodoroc. It was believed that Nodoroc was a sacred (or feared) site to the Creek. According to early reports, the altar (if that's what it was) was located at the western end of the bog. It was a small triangular structure with sides of equal length, roughly twelve feet long and eight feet high, and fashioned out of rough stone. There were indications that it was once covered, perhaps with a thatched bark roof, as many wigwams were. There was a doorway in the wall facing the boiling mud pit. Above the doorway was a stone lintel that jutted out about two feet that showed signs of being used for some kind of ceremonial purpose. The upper side of the stone and the part of the wall facing it had scorch marks, indicating long and repeated action of fires. Inside the western corner of the structure was a stone altar with three steps bearing similar scorch marks as the stone projecting above the doorway. By the time settlers discovered the structure it appeared to have been abandoned for quite some time, as sapling trees had taken root inside. The purpose of the strange stone temple can only be guessed at, or whether or not it was even man-made.

The story of the stone altar is a bit of an enigma. According to archaeologists a structure like that would be completely out of character with the practices of tribes in the area. Unfortunately, it no longer stands at Nodoroc. In 1837 Governor George R. Gilmer (1790-1859) purchased the structure (whatever it was) and had it moved to the front yard of his residence in Lexington, GA. The so-called "altar" became a lawn ornament. The stones are basalt boulders similar to ones found at nearby Fort Yargo State Park. So it's possible they mistook a natural formation for a man-made construction.

The Wog

Legends also state that leaders of the Creek tribe would bring their most heinous criminals to Nodoroc and cast them into the steaming bog where they would endure eternal torment. Allegedly this was done to appease a monstrous creature called the "Wog" that lived in Nodoroc. One story tells of a Creek woman named Fenceruga who murdered and ate her own child. After she was apprehended, Chief Urocasca had her executed by throwing her headfirst into the hottest part of Norodoc. When she struck the mud the Wog appeared. Then, while she struggled in the burning muck, the Wog took its huge tail and swept mud over her, burying her forever in the mire. However, there's one big problem with this part of the legend: the Creeks did not engage in human sacrifices. The tales of human sacrifice were likely made up by storytellers, either European or Creek. It was common for early settlers to attribute all kinds of unspeakable acts of barbarism to indigenous people to add drama to a story and dehumanize them, but it's also possible that it was told by Creek chiefs to scare away European settlers.

The Wog.

Nodoroc was a fearful and dangerous place, but it was the swamp's fabled monstrous inhabitant the Creek and white settlers feared the most. In *The Early History of Jackson County, Georgia*, Wilson writes:

The Wog was said to be a jet-black, long-haired animal about the size of a horse, but his legs were much shorter, the front ones being some twelve inches longer than the hind ones. This gave him something of the appearance of a huge dog "sitting on its tail." And when walking seemed to require him to carry forward one side at a time. His tail was very large, all the way of the same size, and at the end of it there was a bunch of entirely white hair at least eight inches long and larger in diameter than the tail itself. Whether sitting, standing, or walking, this curious appendage was in constant motion from side to side, not as a dog wags its tail, but with a quick upward curve which brought it down with a whizzing sound that could be distinctly heard at least when twenty-five or thirty steps distant. But the most distinguishing feature of this horrid tail was that it revealed the presence of the monster in the dark — the only time he ventured to go abroad. His great red eyes were very repulsive, but not so much so that his forked tongue, the prongs of which were thought to be eight inches long and sometimes played in and out of his mouth like those of a mad snake. Really the meanest feature about the beast was that his bear-like head contained a set of great white teeth over which his ugly lips never closed.

The guards quickly seize their unresisting prisoner, swing him high into the air and let him fall headlong into the blazing lake.

Fabled *Volcano* in Georgia

Others who encountered the Wog had similar descriptions, but it's the creature's strange tail, ending with a white tip shaped like a trowel, that is the most intriguing part. And what do we make of the strange sound it made? When it wagged its tail it would create a strange buzzing or whirring sound that could be heard from a long distance. Black devil-dogs with red eyes, and occasionally forked tongues, show up in many tales of hell-hounds in folklore from Appalachia to the British Isles, but a whirring clubbed tail seems unique. Like the Wog, they too were believed to guard the gateways to the underworld.

The Wog was rumored to eat the corpses of those who perished in Nodoroc. When there weren't enough of those it would stalk the countryside seeking out fresh graves, using its huge paws to dig through the loosened soil, drag out newly buried corpses, and devour them. The Wog didn't attack the living unless it was disturbed. According to C. Fred Ingram's book, *Beadland to Barrow*, the Wog's only mission was to frighten people and animals. Ingram writes, "The early settlers learned from the Indians that if they left him alone he would go away without doing any harm."

The Wog would often show up around people's houses at night, attracted to the light. Nervous animals acting wild and panicked was the first sign the Wog was near. Horses snorted, cattle moaned, and dogs and cats hid themselves. Then there would be the strange whirring sound that removed any shadow of doubt the Wog was paying a visit. If there was a light on, the Wog would stick its long tongue through any opening it could find. The tongue would flicker under doors, and if there were any gaps in a cabin's chinking it would find them and stick its horrible, forked tongue inside, tasting the air like a snake. From within the cabin, one could hear the eerie whirring sound the creature made with its tail as it moved around the house. People would turn out their lights, huddle in the dark, and hope that the Wog would quickly lose interest and go away.

The vast majority of what we know of Nodoroc and the Wog comes from Wilson's 1914 book *The Early History of Jackson County, Georgia*. Unfortunately, he doesn't provide many sources for his material, which wasn't uncommon at the time. We don't know if he got his information through oral traditions, local records, and early pioneer testimonies, or if he just made parts up. Though the book presents itself as a history book, it's really more of a collection of history mixed with dramatized tall tales; as such, it should be taken with a grain of salt, or maybe even an entire salt-lick.

The earliest documented account of the Wog that I can find (though they call it a "Woog") comes from an 1895 article in the *Atlanta Constitution* titled, "This Is a 'Woog' — A New and Terrible Animal in Jackson County". The articles states,

Mr. J. G. Mauldin and Mr. S. P. Millar say that there is a strange animal near Jefferson whose home is on the headwaters of the mile branch. He is a long, keen animal with a long bushy tail, large flat feet, a small, keen neck, little ears and takes nocturnal perambulations through forest and meadow, seeking prey and devouring chickens, sheep, pigs, and things of that kind. He has frightened the people badly over about Mr. Mauldin's and they are almost afraid to venture out at night for fear they will be attacked by the varmint. ... This animal makes a circuit every night and sometimes they say he even roams in the suburbs of our city. The varmint is a strange thing and Billy LeMaster has named it a 'woog.'

The next month, another article ran in the *Atlanta Constitution* titled, "The Jackson County 'Woog' — It's Still at Large and the Good Citizens are Frightened." The article mentions a "woog" that "infests the forests along the meanderings of mile branch". The article continues:

Since the discovery of this new specimen of supposed to be extinct and fossiliferous animal by Messrs. Mauldin and Miller, he has been seen by several other people, and they all have a different description of him. He has been seen by several women and a whole generation of children, and he has on a different suit of clothes and a different look for every one that sees him. Some say that he is long, keen, and stringy, like a grey-hound; others say he somewhat resembles a bear, and walks a good deal of the time on his hind feet alone; a few describe it as being somewhat like an ostrich, while others say it is more like a lion; some give it a sphinx-like appearance that has a face, eyes, mouth, and even whiskers, like a man, while it has seven hairs on its head and a body like a big black dog. It is reported that it can laugh like a man.

Perhaps the "woog" story of 1895 is what gave Wilson the idea for a fictionalized Wog to be included in his book nineteen years later. The part describing the "Woog" as a dog-like creature that "walks a good deal of the time on his hind feet alone" should be interesting to people familiar with recent so-called "Dogman" sightings.

Interestingly, over the years "wog" has become a slang term for "wolf-dog" hybrids, a portmanteau of the words "wolf" and "dog." Perhaps this hints to the origin of the creature's name. Unfortunately, it should also be noted that the term "wog" is a derogatory term used by Brits to describe dark-skinned foreigners.

Nodoroc Today

Nodoroc still exists, though it's no longer a flammable cauldron of boiling mud and foul vapors. A few years ago, I had the opportunity to see Nodoroc for myself. While the bog is only a fraction of its original size it's still a very weird area. What remains of Nodoroc sits within a depression and is fed by natural springs. The low wooded ridges around it give it the impression of being within a crater. Water drains out the eastern side forming a small creek that carves its way through the sodden earth. As I stood on the east bank I tried to imagine what the large stone altar on the opposite side would have looked like, if it ever existed at all. I tried to picture the dark stone with sacrificial fires burning. It's a place that can really get your imagination going.

While the blazing mud and demonic beasts may be long gone, It's still a wild and potentially dangerous place. The peat bog is full of sinkholes and quicksand-like mud. There are areas of solid-looking grassy mats floating on murky water, but they are definitely not solid. One wrong step and you'll be deep in the muck and perhaps meet the same horrible fate as Fenceruga the Cannibal.

I hiked around being mindful of my footing and noted the mud there really does have a blueish-black hue, and that a number of the trees have grown into strange corkscrew patterns. Finally, I found a patch of higher ground overlooking the bog that was dry enough to sit down comfortably and just take the place in. There's a special feeling that legend-trippers get when they're present at an actual legendary site — a certain frisson. Maybe it's the emotional/intellectual version of a runner's high. Things feel paradoxically unreal and hyper-real simultaneously. I found myself looking around thinking, *This is where it all happened. This is the spot.* And even if some of it didn't actually happen exactly as the old tales say it didn't matter. Either way, it was still ground zero for a wonderful legend that has been passed down from generation to generation for over a hundred years.

As I sat there and watched the ferns swaying in the light breeze, I consciously kept my ears open for a sound that might be carried on the breeze; a sound that frightened Creek warriors and turned settlers' blood cold; a strange whirring sound that let me know *the Wog is near.*

Resources and Works Consulted:

Atlanta Constitution. "The Jackson County 'Woog' — It's Still at Large and the Good Citizens Are Frightened." March 4, 1895.

Atlanta Constitution. "This Is a 'Woog' — A New and Terrible Animal in Jackson County." February 18, 1985.

Ingram, C. Fred. *Beadland to Barrow.* Cherokee Pub. Co, 1978.

Weatherly, David. *Peach State Monsters: Cryptids & Legends of Georgia.* Eerie Lights Publishing. 2021.

Wilson, Gustavus James Nash. *The Early History of Jackson County, Georgia.* Foote & Davies Co. 1914.

The Forgotten Wendigo Island
By Chad Lewis

Place names are important. They reflect our shared history, family genealogy, social successes, and our folklore. From the street you live on and the grade school you attended, to the park where you walk your dog, the names of places provide a powerful insight into the past. The idea of giving places specific names wasn't meant just to differentiate between similar landmarks or regions, it was often meant to serve as a remembrance of a person, place, or event. Occasionally these place names were given in order to provide a warning that the location was cursed, dangerous, or sacred. Places like Devil's Swamp in Mississippi or Dead Woman's Crossing in Oklahoma act as a supernatural signpost for those who choose to travel out to them. One perfect example of a place name documenting its odd history is a tiny island tucked away in the Northwoods of Minnesota called Wendigo Island. However, before we delve into the history and folklore of the island, we have to take a slight detour in order to explore what the Wendigo actually is.

The Wendigo is the deadliest and most feared creature (spirit, legend, being) ever to set foot in North America. It began with the First Nations people of Canada, who knew this thing by many different names and spellings. The legend of the Wendigo quickly spread throughout the wilds of Canada, while also making its way to the Great Lakes and Northeast portions of the United States. The legend is so ancient that many indigenous cultures do not know where it originated, it has always just been there. The Wendigo could show up in physical form to attack and devour you. It was always said to be immense---somewhere around eight-feet tall and as large as it wanted to be. Witnesses often told of it being taller than the tallest trees. Traditionally it was depicted as being thin and skeletal, its rough skin pulled tight over its emaciated body. Sometimes it is spotted with its lips and mouth torn away because it has an insatiable hunger for human flesh and when no prey (you and me) is around it will resort to eating its own body in order to survive. The more it devours, the larger it becomes. The modern depiction of the Wendigo as having giant elk-like antlers or strange looking horns did not start to appear until the 1940s. Worse yet, the Wendigo could show up in a spirit form and slowly start to possess you---turning you into a Wendigo. The good news is that up until the point where you fully transform into the Wendigo, you can be cured through several different means. However, once you have fully become a Wendigo, death is your only means of escape.

The mere mention of these monsters was enough to strike absolute terror, chaos, and panic into the very fabric of early First Nations and pioneer life, often forcing peoples to abandon their communities until the deadly beasts had passed by. The fear of a Wendigo is so colossal, it caused people to do strange things. To illustrate this point, here is a short excerpt from the book *Wendigo Lore* that I co-wrote in 2020 with my colleague Kevin Lee Nelson, which featured the fear that accompanied the Wendigo:

In 1932, the *Brandon Daily Sun* reported "28 Cree Indians driven from their trapping grounds by superstitious fear of their god Wendigo." Fearing the Wendigo, the tribe left their grounds and headed north only to find themselves without any game due to the Wendigo's curse. As they slowly marched North in search of game, their health deteriorated and one by one the tribe perished in the unforgiving conditions. The lone survivor relayed the tragic story to the trappers he encountered.

These people had not spotted the Wendigo approaching their lodging grounds, they did not hear the Wendigo making its way toward them, they merely heard a rumor that the Wendigo was nearby, so they abandoned their encampment and set off toward death and starvation. That is how powerful the belief in the Wendigo is.

Wendigo Island sits in the middle of a small bay off of Pokegama Lake called Wendigo Arm Bay, which is located just south of the town of Grand Rapids, Minnesota. The triangle shaped island itself is relatively small, consisting of just over one acre of land. In the 1950s, the island was unofficially known as "Emerald Island" and housed Camp Mishawaka, a summer camp for local youths. It is theorized that the camp counselors and campers heard the grisly legend of the island and renamed it Wendigo Island.

From the earliest settlement days, the pioneers believed the island was important to the native peoples. In 2023, the Itasca County History Society in Grand Rapids, Minnesota, sent me a file that contained a hand-typed chapter called Part IV The Ojibwa Making Connections: Wendigo. In this fascinating history of the land, the researcher, shares a story from the early pioneer, Willis Mason West, who stated that "his family would sometimes hear the chanting of a procession of birch bark canoes, making their way to Windago Island." The family would watch from shore at "a respectful distance,,.,ancient rituals of the Chippewa who had paddled far to retain this fragment of their culture on Windago Island." West also stated that

Wendigo Island "is where they buried the dead of the outcast of the tribe." Several other people mentioned that the island is where the outcasts were buried, yet not one of them expounded on what constituted an outcast. West also expressed his disappointment and sadness over finding depressions in the high ground of the island where "random grave robbers had taken their bones and offerings to their gods." In 1994, West also interviewed a 95-year-old man who had lived in a cabin on Pokegama Lake in the 1920s. The man was very familiar with the local Ojibwe people and stated "Wendigo Island was kind of a weird place for the Indians. They didn't like it. They were afraid of it." The problem with all this information is that I cannot locate the book/pamphlet/paper which the chapter was taken from. Of course, I emailed the historical society and asked for the source of the document so I could cite it. After a couple weeks went by without word, I called the historical society and they informed me that my source request has piqued their interest because they cannot find where the material came from. They have scoured their historical books and local writings but have so far come up empty-handed. At the time of this printing, they are still actually trying to locate where this mysterious chapter came from.

In 1935, numerous newspapers throughout the Midwest published an article about the research of George Galbreath, in which the November 24 edition of the *Minneapolis Journal* called him "One of the most informed men on the habits, customs and language of the Chippewa Indians." The September 26 edition of the *Grand Rapids Herald-Review* featured Galbreath opining on Wendigo Island's origin, stating, "Indian children were warned of an evil spirit, which liked nothing better than to devour bad little girls and boys. For some reason Indians living near Pokegama Lake had this Wendago living on an island in the east part of the lake, hence Wendago Island, Wendago Park, and Wendago School."

In 1996, in a reply to a request for information on Wendigo Island from Professor West, Earl Nyhom, a Professor of Ojibwe at Bemidji State University told that the "Wiindigoo is the winter cannibal of Ojibwe legends," and that it "dwells under the ice in winter. Sometimes during the coldest time of the winter, when the ice is heard cracking on the lake, that sound is said to be the sound of the Wiindigoo coming through the ice." I found this belief to be especially interesting as it rings similar to another Wendigo legend involving a place called Lake Wendigo on Star Island just east of Bemidji, Minnesota. At this lake, there are tales of people discovering large holes in the frozen ice with huge footprints walking away from the hole toward the island as the Wendigo came up out of the icy water and made its way to the island in search of fresh prey.

You might be saying to yourself that as spooky as this all sounds, it is nothing more than superstition from hundreds of years ago. Today we have nothing to be fearful of. If you fall under this line of thinking, you would be wrong. A few years ago, I traveled to the Cass Lake region of Minnesota to give a lecture on mysterious creatures of the area for the local public middle/high school system. Before I even began my talk, several tribal elders approached me with a request. They told me that they had heard I was going to speak about a certain feared creature that was said to roam the area. Although they dared not even speak the name of the Wendigo, I knew exactly what legend they were referring to. The fear of saying the name of a creature or monster stems from the belief that merely mentioning the name of a legend is enough to put you on its radar, and once it knows who and where you are, it will come looking for you. I have found this to be a nearly universal fear as I have encountered this among locals of nearly every country I have visited.

Over my three decades of research, I have learned that if you expect various communities to open up and share their long-held stories and legends with you, you need to respect local traditions and beliefs, regardless of whether or not you share those beliefs. Obviously, I told the elders that I would certainly remove the unnamed legend from my program. My words had no sooner left my mouth when I saw their body language immediately relax as though some great fear had instantaneously dissipated. At least for the next few hours, we would all be safe from the Wendigo.

In the 1970s, there were several archeological digs on the that island turned up countless pieces of human remains from the discarded burial ground, even with a long history of grave robbers operating on the island. Today, Wendigo Island is privately owned. However, it is still easily visible from the public shoreline where you can view the island from a respectable distance just like the early pioneers did almost 200 years ago. Winter also provides you with the opportunity to transverse the frozen over waters of the bay, thereby giving you a closer opportunity to scout out the island. If you do choose to try your luck on the ice, be on the lookout for giant holes in the ice where the Wendigo might just be waiting for you.

Resources and Works Consulted:

Brandon Daily Sun. October 28, 1932.

Grand Rapids Herald-Review. September 26, 1935.

Lewis, Chad & Nelson, Kevin Lee. Wendigo Lore: Monsters, Myths, and Madness. On the Road Publications. 2020.

The Offbeat Track:
The Miracle Dirt of Chimayo
By David Weatherly

Chimayo is a small, census-designated place in New Mexico's Rio Arriba and Santa Fe Counties. With just over three thousand residents, the village itself is a welcoming place with pleasant people surrounded by stunning northern New Mexican scenery. The little community is also home to a curious attraction—an old church with purportedly magical dirt that draws people from all over the world who seek its healing power.

Commonly known as El Santuario de Chimayo, the church was built in 1816 by Bernardo de la Encarnacion Abeyta. The legend of the site's magic goes back much further though, and there are different magical tales connected to the site.

Some accounts claim that the Tewa tribe who once lived in the area considered the land sacred for its healing powers. The Catholic legend began in the early 1800s. Popular lore says that in 1810, a friar named Abeyta was performing penances in Chimayo when he saw a light bursting from a nearby hillside. Digging in the area, the man discovered a crucifix that he dubbed "Our Lord of Esquipulas."

A priest named Fr. Alvarez took the crucifix to Santa Cruz, but once he installed it there, it vanished, only to reappear back in the hole in New Mexico where it had first been found. This occurred two more times, and after the third magical relocation of the crucifix, the message got through—the item was to remain in Chimayo.

A variation of the story connected to the site deals with the same friar, Bernardo de la Encarnacion Abeyta. Abeyta was reportedly watching his sheep and contemplating his life. He was sick at the time and was praying to his patron saint, San Esquipulas. Abeyta had a vision of the saint and followed the figure's beckoning hand. When Abeyta knelt at the spot the saint indicated he was immediately healed. Afterwards, out of gratitude, Abeyta built a chapel on the spot.

Shortly after the chapel was built, people started reporting miraculous healings. There was so much activity at the site, and so many reported cures, that a larger chapel was built in 1816, what is now the Chimayo shrine and adobe mission.

The church was owned privately for many years, but in 1929, descendants were having financial problems and sold the site to a group of preservationists—the Spanish Colonial Arts Society. The group promptly donated the property to the Catholic Archdiocese of Santa Fe which owns it to this day. El Santuario de Chimayo was declared a National Historic Landmark in 1970.

Known as the "Lourdes of America," people come from all over the world in hopes of experiencing a healing miracle. The mysterious crucifix is still in the chapel—resting in a place of prominence on the altar.

Curiously, the crucifix itself isn't the focus of the purported healings; rather, the miracle is said to come from a "sacred sand pit" located behind the main altar.

The sand comes from a hole, purportedly the original spot where the crucifix was discovered. Next to the room where the pit lies is the Prayer Room, an area filled with items discarded by those who say they were cured after standing in the pit of sacred dirt. Old crutches, braces and other items are routinely left in the church by those who struggled in their journey to the site but left unencumbered by their previous physical ailments or restrictions. Letters asking for blessings and healing are also left at the site.

The dirt is commonly rubbed on the body, sometimes on the areas specifically wounded or suffering, though in the past, some people would eat the dirt in order to take in its healing powers.

It's also common for people to leave photographs of family members in the prayer room, typically family members who need healing. On one of my trips, I saw a woman taking dirt from the hole and rubbing it on a photograph of her son.

Many people also just keep the dirt, placing it on home altars, or in small items they wear or keep on their persons. Of course, the church itself doesn't comment on the purported healing properties or the reported miracles that have occurred at the sanctuary.

The chapel has become a modern pilgrimage site and receives around 300,000 visitors each year. It is, in fact, noted as the most important Catholic pilgrimage center in the United States. Holy Week sees the highest number of visitors with the biggest crowds arriving on Holy Thursday and Good Friday and a large percentage of the people who make the pilgrimage walk—some from as far away as Santa Fe or even Albuquerque—about ninety miles away.

The best time to stop at Chimayo for a low-key visit is on a weekday during the mid-morning or afternoon hours. Although the site always has some visitors, this will give you the smallest crowd and make it easier to spend time looking over the various things to see at the site. Be sure to check the site's schedule if you want to avoid any large events.

The feast of Our Lord of Esquipulas is celebrated on January 15 or on the Sunday nearest to that date; and the fourth weekend of July—the feast of St. James the Great—is equally busy, so bear this in mind when planning a stop.

I Dare You: Black Agnes:
The Death Dealer of Vermont
By Chad Lewis

I have always had a fondness and curiosity for graveyard statuary, particularly those that are thought to be haunted, cursed, possessed, or even a portal to a different world. I have been intrigued by the idea that a grave statue---one that is meant to mark a person's eternal resting place, a symbol of their death---can ironically take on a life of its own. As I travel the world in search of the strange and unusual, I always keep my eyes and ears peeled for any dares that may be associated with cemetery statues. I have found that the overwhelming majority of these dares are negative in nature. If you complete the dare---mishap, misfortune, or even death will soon follow. For some, it is precisely the inherent danger that accompanies these dares that makes them so appealing. If you like to tempt fate and live dangerously, let me introduce you to Black Agnes.

In Montpelier, Vermont, lies the historic Green Mount Cemetery. This hillside burial spot is overflowing with elaborate mausoleum monuments and beautifully ornate grave statues. Everywhere you turn in this graveyard you are confronted by remarkable works of cemetery art. Yet, among all the spectacular statuary, one piece stands out from the rest---it is a forlorn looking statue watching over the grave of John Hubbard, a statue that has come to be known as Black Agnes.

Nearly every legend about John Hubbard tells of his being a nasty person--greedy, mean- spirited, shady, and uncaring. Even his substantial wealth, which he inherited from his aunt (after contesting her will which originally left almost everything to benefit the city) could not make him likable. When death greeted him at the age of 53, the executors of his estate commissioned Karl Bitter to construct his grave's central structure. Finding inspiration from the William Cullen Bryant poem Thanatopsis (Thoughts on Death), the bronze figure he created was meant to represent death itself.

As is true with many bizarre dares, there seems to be some confusion as to what actually needs to be done in order to feel the wrath of the cursed statue. In 1981, *The Times Argus* ran an article on June 10, that told, "if you sit on her lap at midnight you will die in three days." In a *Burlington Free Press* article from September 16, 1994, Vermont author Joseph Citro told the newspaper, "Apparently there's a curse connected to the gravestone for it is said that anyone who sits on Black Agnes's lap in the light of the full moon will suffer seven years of bad luck—and maybe death." In 2006, the *Rutland Daily Herald* added another twist to the legend, stating, "Any brave (or foolish) soul who dares to sit on Black Agne's lap at midnight on Halloween night will,,,oh, the outcome is too terrible to print." Luckily, the article was published on October 29, providing plenty of time for those itching to visit the afterlife to make their way to the cemetery on Halloween night. During my visit to the cemetery, I was told that merely touching the statue, much less sitting on it, could trigger a tsunami of ill-fate.

In addition to the confusion about what to do, there is also some mix-up as to what the statue actually is. In 1996, the *Brattleboro Reformer* helped perpetuate one the most erroneous parts of the legend in their October 30 edition which stated, "Don't sit on the bronze statue of the Virgin Mary." Due in part to the feminine look of the figure, many visitors incorrectly believe that the statue depicts the Virgin Mary, and by sitting on her lap, you are offending Jesus—therefore you will be cursed. I have to admit that this is a unique and imaginative version of the cursed statue.

Regardless of who or what the eerie statue is meant to represent, bad things seem to befall those who press their luck and sit on its lap. Folklore from the surrounding area is filled with tales of supposed car crashes, terrible breakups with significant others, loss of employment, unexplained accidents, and untimely deaths from those who took the dare and lived (or didn't) to tell the tale. Whether you touch the statue, sit on its lap, or heck—even sleep on it, you best have your affairs in order.

Resources and Works Consulted:

Brattleboro Reformer. October 30. 1996.

Burlington Free Press. September 16, 1994.

Rutland Daily Herald. October 29, 2006.

The Times Argus. June 10, 1981.

Disclaimer

The "I Dare You" column and its challenges are presented for educational and entertainment purposes only. The authors, publisher, and Back Roads Lore will not be liable for any harm or injury of any kind to, or death of, any persons or for the damage to, or destruction or loss of any items or property whether caused by gross negligence of the owners, its employees, agents, contractors, or any other persons, of anyone attempting said dares or other challenges or for any other reasons associated with this publication.

I Dare You: Black Agnes: The Death Dealer of Vermont By Chad Lewis

Dedication

This issue of the journal is dedicated to:

Horatio Nelson Jackson (1872-1955)
–The First Person to Drive Across the Country.

A true pioneer of adventure, Horatio Jackson was out driving on the backroads at a time when, for much of the country, the only roads were backroads. In 1903, Horatio Jackson, a medical doctor who did not even own a car, made a $50 bet that he could drive across the entire United States. Accompanied by his mechanic, Sewall Crocker, Jackson left San Francisco and headed off across the wilds of the country. In Idaho, the pair picked up a bulldog named Bud to join their adventure. The image of Bud wearing specially fitted goggles to keep the dust and dirt out of his eyes became the expedition's unofficial flag.

Plagued by faulty equipment that was ill-equipped to handle the rough terrain, inadequate maps and directions, and a series of never-ending setbacks, it is truly amazing that in a mere 63 days on the road the team of adventurers successfully rolled into New York. When all was said and done, the trip consumed 800 gallons of gas and cost Jackson a total of $8,000, which he paid for out of his own pocket. Proving that Jackson mounted this expedition only for the exhilarating adventure it would bring, legend has it that he never collected on the $50 bet.

BACK ROADS LORE

The Back Roads Lore Team

David Weatherly

is known as the renaissance man of the strange and supernatural. Author, adventurer, magician and more, he has traveled the world in search of mysteries. From dusty castles to strange, remote islands and ancient sites, he has journeyed to the most unusual places on the globe seeking the unknown.

Kevin Lee Nelson

is an author, researcher, and adventurer. He has written and lectured on topics of the paranormal, folklore, and the occult for over twenty years. A nomad at heart, Kevin spends much of his time roaming America's back roads in his black muscle car hunting down strange legends and mysterious encounters.

Chad Lewis is an author,

researcher, and lecturer on topics of the strange and unusual. With an academic background in the field of psychology, Chad has traveled the world in search of the supernatural. The more bizarre the legend is, the more likely you will find Chad there.

Made in the USA
Monee, IL
02 March 2024

53979358R00095